HOW TO

KICK THE HABIT!

The Drug Withdrawal Handbook

HOW TO

KICK THE HABIT!

The Drug Withdrawal Handbook

by

C. J. Alexander, M.D., *and*
Sandy Alexander

With a foreword by
JERRY FINKELSTEIN
Publisher: New York Law Journal

FREDERICK FELL, INC.
New York
BOOK PUBLISHERS

"Unhooking Addicts" by Jerry Finkelstein reprinted by permission of The New York Times.
Copyright © 1971 by The New York Times Company.

Copyright © 1972 by Clifton J. Alexander and Sandy Alexander

All Rights Reserved
For Information Address:
Frederick Fell, Inc.
386 Park Avenue South
New York, N.Y. 10016

Library of Congress Card No. 72-175424

SBN 8119-0208-0

Published Simultaneously in Canada by

George J. McLeod, Limited, Toronto 2B, Ontario

MANUFACTURED IN THE UNITED STATES OF AMERICA

To our mother
for her understanding, advice,
and encouragement

ACKNOWLEDGMENTS

We would, at this time, like to take the opportunity to thank the individuals who continue to be so helpfully involved in this critical problem of drug addiction.

We wish to express our gratitude to United States Senators Barry Goldwater, Paul Fannin and Congressman Morris Udall of Arizona and United States Senator Alan Cranston of California—who—as officials of the United States Government—helped us to obtain research data for this book, and displayed such sincere interest in the progress of the methadone program for the treatment of drug addiction.

We are equally indebted to Dr. Allen J. Enclow, Professor and Chairman of the Department of Psychiatry, College of Human Medicine, Michigan State University; Dr. Jay Levenson, Department of Psychiatry, College of Medicine, University of Arizona; and Dr. Donald H. Naftulin, Department of Psychiatry, School of Medicine, University of Southern California; as well as Tucson pathologists Louis Hirsch and Edward A. Brucker, for valuable advice concerning drug analysis and detection.

We are grateful also to Mrs. Marilyn Drago, Medical Editor of the *Arizona Republic;* the library staff of the University of Arizona, College of Medicine; Arizona State Senator and Mrs. William Jacquin; Judge

Lawrence Howard of the Superior Court of Arizona; and Mr. John Fairbank, Senator Cranston's Field Representative.

We sincerely appreciate the enthusiasm of the many patients and former addicts we interviewed for this book, and have attempted to follow their good advice to "tell it as it is."

Our sincere thanks also to Mrs. Henriette Neatrour, our literary agent, for her patience and understanding; and Mr. Peter Kirkland for guidance and suggestions toward finalizing the material in this book. We acknowledge with equal thanks the legal advice given during the preparation of this manuscript by our lawyer and good friend, Ben Lazarow.

We must give credit to Mr. Colin Leinster, Bureau Chief of *Life* Magazine in Chicago, Illinois, for really starting it all. His article, "Life on Two Grams a Day," was featured in the February 20, 1970 issue of *Life* and when it became known that Bill Eppridge's excellent photos had been taken in Dr. Alexander's office, many patients asked for a book that would give all the facts, one that they could give their families in order to establish some kind of mutual communication.

We have tried to help bridge that communication gap.

C.J.A.
S.A.

Tucson, Arizona

A dramatic advertisement appeared in a recent issue of The New York Times, with the headline: U.S. DECLARES WAR ON DRUGS.

The ad went on to say: "That headline hasn't been written yet."

But it better be, soon!

Because nothing short of all out war against drugs can save this nation.

All out mobilization of very single available American resource from brains to dollars that would dwarf even the "Manhattan Project," or the efforts of NASA. Leave no doubt—none—that the White House and Congress, American business, labor and the American public must assign #1 Priority to the complete and utter defeat of drug abuse.

Yes, Priority One.

Because the seeds of our national destruction have already been sown.

Courts clogged with addict cases.

Alienation.

Sub Cultures.

Degradation.

The Fall of Rome.

Any thinking person recognizes the same "clear and present danger" that we do, of course.

The problem is what, if anything, can any one human being, one newspaper, or magazine, or radio, or television station do about it.

Jerry Finkelstein, publisher of the New York Law Journal, wasn't sure either, but he was convinced that something must be done and done now.

So, he wrote a front-page editorial on the subject that appeared in The New York Law Journal, under the headline:

"NEEDED: 'ANOTHER MANHATTAN PROJECT' TO SOLVE NATION'S DRUG PROBLEM."

Then, he prepared an article entitled "UNHOOKING ADDICTS" which was published in The New York Times, opposite the editorial page, that brought the problem into even sharper focus.

Response to the article was instant and overwhelming in calls, wires, letters from Senators, Congressmen, educators, clergymen, and criminologists.

From judges, lawyers, doctors, police.

From parents to corporate presidents.

From publishers, editors, newscasters and columnists —all endorsing the "total war" concept—all pledging personal help and support to keep the movement going. And growing.

That's why we, at Frederick Fell, determined to reprint the article "UNHOOKING ADDICTS" in a book that we were preparing and which you are now reading, entitled HOW TO KICK THE HABIT by Clifton J. Alexander and Sandy Alexander. As Jerry Finkelstein said in his ad, "The time is short. The fuse is burning."

Sincerely,
THE EDITORS

UNHOOKING ADDICTS

By Jerry Finkelstein

Publisher: New York Law Journal

An astronaut, back from the moon, displays symptoms of an unknown disease. The disease spreads, killing many and permanently disabling most of those who contract it. What comes next?

Any science fiction fan knows that the President declares a national emergency and appoints a czar with plenary powers to meet the threat.

Men, money and materials would be co-opted.

Red tape would dissolve.

All who could conceivably contribute to solving the problems would do so, willy-nilly.

The Manhattan Project, the New Deal and the space program would be dwarfed by comparison. And the finest minds, backed by the resources and power of our country, would solve the problems. The threat would be overcome.

That is fantasy. But is reality better? We have our own mutating Andromeda Strain in the opiates, barbiturates, amphetamines and hallucinogens. Cocaine has re-emerged and laboratories are inventing synthetics and derivatives faster than they can be outlawed. Instead of infection we have addiction.

Our present Andromeda Strain did not come from the moon or outer space. It comes from the poppy fields of Turkey via the laboratories of Marseilles, the hemp fields of Mexico, the chemical laboratories of great universities and from dozens of other sources. It is spread by human rats and lice rather than more primitive vectors. It does not kill quickly and cleanly nor disable neatly and tidily. It also degrades.

It is unnecessary to dwell on the scope of the drug crisis. Anyone- who needs to be convinced that there is a drug epidemic must be a newly trained translator in Peking.

What do we actually have to meet the drug crisis? Piecemeal programs and miniscule financing. Temporizing statements and dangerous panaceas.

The lack of basic research is frightening. We know more about moon rocks than marijuana. Is it dangerous or not? Should we legalize it or class it with the hard drugs? Ironically, the only answer given as to why marijuana and other hallucinogens should not be legalized comes not from science but from history. Only two societies tolerated the widespread use of hallucinogens: the Arab, which then managed to turn the most fertile part of its world into a desert; and peyote-chewing tribes, whose noblest hour came as their hearts were ripped out as human sacrifices to foreign gods.

As to hard drugs, a current palliative is methadone, which, like heroin, is a derivative of opium. Even as a palliative, this is inadequate; and we must heed the nagging memory that the original use for heroin, as the authority Hindesmith notes, was "as a non-habit-form-

12

ing substitute for opium or morphine or as a cure for drug addiction."

What is urgently needed is a strongly financed, well-coordinated mobilization of the nation's resources to develop a comprehensive program to put an end to this national disaster and disgrace.

The United States has attacked many difficult problems and found solutions through massive injections of money and talent. Drug abuse should be approached in the same manner.

Why haven't the obvious steps been taken?

Cost should be no consideration. The Manhattan Project produced the atomic bomb—and radioactive isotopes are a mainstay of modern medicine.

The space program put men on the moon—and whole industries produce undreamt of products (including advanced prosthetics) as a result.

Can one conceive of the potential by-products of the war on addiction? Wholly apart from the heartbreak tragedies prevented, the crime and corruption uprooted, and the malaise of fear eliminated, we can predict priceless discoveries in biochemistry, psychology and many other fields.

Who would oppose any remotely reasonable steps taken?

Industrialists with billions lost annually from lowered productivity, absenteeism and theft?

Unions with their members fearful for their children?

Farmers with the infection now spreading to the most remote communities?

Churches?

Blacks?

Judges and lawyers?

Physicians?

Shopkeepers?

Liberals?

Conservatives?

Only organized crime would oppose a war on addiction.

How old are your daughters and granddaughters? I have two granddaughters and hope for more. I would revere any man who could wipe out addiction—and so would you.

Polio crippled, but it did not debase. Cancer kills, but it does not degrade.

We honored Drs. Salk and Sabin for conquering polio. A greater mantle awaits the conqueror of cancer.

Why has no one made a name for himself as Mr. Anti-Addiction? Is it because the job of making any serious impact is too great for anyone but the President of the United States?

The President has a unique opportunity. Already, with the freeze, he has established that he has the capacity for taking drastic action, together with the ability to accept ideas from others regardless of party. I pray that he will use his great powers against the common enemy of mankind and start to vanquish drug addiction now. We can't wait.

Contents

Part I: The Doctor's Rx

16

Part II: Tell Me, Doctor!

The purpose of this book is to make available to teen-agers, their parents, their friends, and all concerned individuals the truth about the dangers of drug addiction, as well as the newest means of combating the use of deadly drugs that has reached epidemic proportions in our society.

PART I

● ● ● ●

The Doctor's Rx

CHAPTER I

THE KILLER DRUGS:

What You Should Know About Their Use

● ● ● ●

The new life-style . . . The heroin story . . . The case
against marijuana . . . The first role of the parent
. . . Who will help . . .

Youth's addiction to the "hard drugs" has reached the
proportions of an epidemic. At this writing, it is estimated that as many as 20 percent of our teen-age gen-
eration is already "hooked." Some of these young
men and women will die soon after addiction from a
self-administered overdose. Those that survive will be
permanently damaged by their tragic dependence upon
drugs. Never again will they have complete control and
coordination of their minds and bodies because of their
enslavement to the "habit."

This seeming defiance of convention and desire for
adventure into the unknown can only lead to such
tragic, fatal consequences. What frequently starts as a
lark too often begins a life of agony and despair. The
most frequent question that arises now is, why drug
usage by the rich and the poor, by youngsters of all
ethnic and cultural backgrounds, so menacingly appears on our present-day scene.

The new life-style

The many reasons why our children are turning to drugs will be discussed in more detail in the following chapters. However, one explanation proffered over and over again by young addicts is that it is considered "the thing to do in order to make the scene," to be accepted by their peers, their schoolmates and the other youngsters of their group. It may start with the smoking of a marijuana "baby" or "reefer," and then, when the thrill of that has vanished, continue with "coffee," which in the language of their way of life refers to LSD. When that no longer seems to suffice, the next step is mainlining "henry," or heroin, into the bloodstream. By that time the thrill-seeking adventure has turned into addiction and the miserable, agonizing existence that means being hooked. Only immediate help from medical experts can prevent more fatal consequences.

The purpose of this book is not to moralize, but rather to explain all the available facts concerning the dangerous use of hard drugs and thereby enable each reader to evaluate his own situation in the light of that information. Many things that we take for granted in our present life-style are addictive. Tranquilizers, sleeping pills, coffee, cigarettes, even aspirin can be habit forming. Sufferers from the myriad illnesses of mankind often unknowingly become dependent on pain relievers.

History from time immemorial has recorded man's addiction to alcohol, various herbs, and other drug forms. These are props, used to create a temporary feeling of artificial well-being that would otherwise be absent. This is especially true of individuals who are tired, bored, depressed. These people seek some form of release from those of their problems that are difficult to manage. Most traditionally, this release is alcohol. However, in some areas, drugs have been used instead. Hashish, the pure resinous exudate of the female hemp plant, has been cultivated and used in Turkey and the Middle East for centuries. Its usage spread from there to the rest of the world.

The heroin story

Toward the end of the nineteenth century, pure forms of narcotics were synthesized for medical use by European chemists. In this manner, heroin was developed from the base of the opium poppy. The name "heroin" is derived from the German word *heroisch,* meaning large or powerful; it is referred to chemically as diacetylmorphine hydrochloride. This is a semisynthetic derivative of morphine obtained by the action of acetic anhydride or acetylchloride on morphine. The result is a white, odorless, bitter-tasting crystalline powder that is soluble in water. (Mexican heroin is brown.) In 1898 in Germany, the Bayer Company developed heroin as an analgesic more potent than morphine for use as a highly effective cough suppressant. Upon discovery that heroin relieved the symptoms of morphine withdrawal, it was administered as a cure for addiction to morphine. Heroin, at that time, was considered nonaddictive. Twelve years later, physicians discovered that heroin was even more addictive than morphine!

In 1924 the United States Congress passed a law prohibiting the manufacture, possession, sale, or use of heroin in the United States. Further regulations enacted in 1956 by the United States Government required immediate surrender to the Federal authorities of all existing stocks of heroin in the possession of drug manufacturers, pharmacies, and physicians. The United Nations instituted similar action to discourage the use of heroin. By 1963 it was imported and used medically in only five countries and manufactured in only three. Although the use of heroin in medicine is now forbidden by law in the United States, it is still legally prescribed in Great Britain. Some British physicians believe that there is no medication as effective as heroin in the treatment of intractable pain.

Heroin has provided many ill-advised users with a means of achieving temporary freedom from care, responsibility, and their meaningful place in society. But they soon find that this habit leads to another kind of enslavement, an existence dependent upon the next "fix." That next fix is a must for the heroin user. At first, one injection a day suffices; then two, three, four, five, or even six are vital to the addict's survival, for the heroin addict soon becomes the victim of his own vice. Many of them tell themselves at the start that they will try one fix for "kicks" and then leave the stuff alone. However, almost always, they are trapped after the first "hit." They then try a second fix just to prove to themselves that they can take it or leave it alone. Instead, all too often, they discover that they are hopelessly addicted; what had started out as an experience now becomes a deadly and costly habit.

The case against marijuana

Involvement can occur in many ways. Curiosity and pressure by other members of their group at school or in the neighborhood frequently lead youngsters to experiment with drugs. Too often, this starts with smoking a reefer of marijuana. Although some pharmacologists state that smoking marijuana—the flowering tops, stems, and leaves of the female Indian hemp plant—is not habit forming, statistics of the United States Public Health Service tend to show that there is a degree of toxicity and that there may be some permanent brain damage to smokers. The next experiment is with mescaline and peyote-hallucinogenic products of the cactus plants. When that thrill lessens, they go on to drugs such as "speed," a form of amphetamine.

All too often, these youthful thrill seekers become so jaded that the repeated use of "pot" no longer has any satisfactory effect. This widespread use of drugs is practiced by the youth of all income groups throughout the country. In the East, youngsters from wealthy families as well as those from minority groups indulge in drug experimentation to such a large extent that it has reached dangerous proportions. In New York City, of a total figure of nine hundred fatalities due to heroin, 224 were teen-agers who had died from overdoses. According to a recent article in *Time* Magazine, there may be as many as twenty-five thousand young addicts in New York City alone! Heroin addiction of users less than twenty-five years of age is believed by Federal authorities to have increased 40 percent from 1968 to 1969. Figures for drug usage have increased alarmingly

27

in the Midwest, South, Far West, and Pacific Coast as well within the past year.

The first role of the parent

Unfortunately, acquiring this drug habit is much simpler than becoming free of its hold upon mind and body. That is why it is extremely important for the parents of drug users to never berate their children or lose their "cool." It will only create a deeper wedge of misunderstanding and further widen the rift between parent and youngster. Communication, understanding, and assistance are essential for both the addict and his family if the drug user is to be helped. Every effort should be made by the *parents to gain their child's confidence and trust.* This is vital in establishing a bridge of communication that will permit the necessary medical and psychiatric treatment to be instituted at the earliest possible moment in order to reverse the life-endangering effects of these dangerous drugs.

If the pupils of your youngster's eyes suddenly become pinpoint and are widely dilated or glazed, if he seems to be unusually nervous or tense and disappears for considerable lengths of time for no apparent reason, or you observe telltale needle marks on his arms or legs, don't—however shocking this discovery may be—reach for the panic button!

Calmly, attempt to discuss the situation with your youngster. Show that you really care. It is imperative that you make every effort to help find a constructive way out of the torture chamber of drug enslavement before irrevocable tragedy strikes. The drug user who is treated with contempt by his family will never respond to therapy. Empathy and trust must be established between the addict and his family before it can be achieved with a therapist. The physicians who are specially trained in this treatment must have the complete confidence and cooperation of the drug user. Without such complete faith on the part of the addict, nothing worthwhile or lasting can be achieved.

Who will help

It is vital that parents frankly discuss with their youngsters the need for immediate treatment by such physicians skilled in the management of these problems. If you suspect drug addiction in your family or a friend, it is imperative that the family physician examine the patient thoroughly at the earliest possible moment. The physician will check for those telltale needle marks on the individual's arms, legs, toes, and the cartoid artery in the neck area.

If you do not have a family physician, it is suggested that you contact your local medical society or hospital for the names of several physicians skilled in the treatment of drug addiction. When arranging an appointment, you should discuss the problem frankly. Ask the doctor to confirm whether or not he is trained in that specialization. If his reply is negative, request the names of physicians versed in these problems and the addict's special needs for professional treatment and understanding.

Please remember, at this critical time it is essential that you render and accept all the necessary help without indulging in self-pity. You must assist the patient on the long, arduous road back to recovery, and it's up to you to inspire confidence and set an example of self-assurance and helpfulness in every possible manner.

You must show that you really care what happens to your youngster. Your love and desire to help will create a bridge of understanding that will give the young drug user the will to "kick the habit" and, with the proper medical treatment, achieve a clean bill of health.

CHAPTER II

THE SYMPTOMS:

How You Can Recognize a Drug User and His Drug

● ● ● ●

The first signs of drug usage . . . The amphetamine addict . . . The glue sniffer . . . The cocaine user . . . The heroin habit . . . The "acid head" . . . The mind distorters . . .

We are fortunate that we are now equipped with effective preventive measures against dangerous drug addiction. The tragedy is that all too often parents, family, and friends do not recognize the first telltale symptoms of drug usage and are usually the last to know. Time and again, I hear young people in my office complain, "If only my folks would have been interested enough to notice that I was stoned and wobbling around the house."

The first signs of drug usage

Alicia, a sixteen-year-old former high-school majorette put it very aptly when she said: "I hoped my parents would have noticed that I wasn't interested in school activities any more. I wanted them to ask me what was happening. They just didn't seem to care until I got busted by the fuzz for shooting scag. Maybe they still didn't care when that happened, but they were ashamed of having their friends know that their daughter was hooked on heroin and insisted I come here for treatment. I still am not sure about their feelings toward me. But I am glad it happened that way. It gave me a chance to meet with other kids like me at Awareness House. We communicate and share experiences. This makes all the difference in changing our life-styles. It's hard to kick the stuff when you are a loner!"

The best time to stop drug abuse is before it starts. However, unfortunately, this is not always possible, simply because the drug user will attempt by all means possible to hide his or her habit. You must be alert to the first indications of drug dependence. You cannot simply ignore the symptoms and expect them to vanish. You must be watchful for changes in the physical appearance as well as the personality of the individual. If faced immediately, directly, and openly at home, the problems of prevention, though difficult for the family, are far simpler than the heartbreak of a late attempt to cure a long-standing addiction.

All too frequently drug abusers are victims of their own misgivings. They seek to stifle their own doubts, lack of confidence, and fears by an artificially induced state of euphoria. Although it is heroin addiction that is now at epidemic levels in this country and throughout the world, other drugs equally addictive and dangerous are being used widely by young people and mature adults.

The user almost always convinces himself that he is

taking the drug—be it "bennies" (benzadrine) or a "cube" (a sugar cube with LSD)—to create additional energy or staying power for a particular situation. Students and long-distance truckdrivers frequently resort to bennies to keep awake. Others may use acid to allegedly free their minds for artistic projects such as paintings and musical compositions by means of hallucinations that all too often become recurring nightmares. There are many such addictive drugs that individuals use to create unusual and often bizarre results. Once the user is dependent on the drug for any purpose, he is enslaved by the self-destructive habit.

The amphetamine addict

Amphetamines are synthetic amines with a stimulating effect on the central nervous system of the user. Prolonged usage can produce irreversible damage and death. When these drugs are taken properly under expert medical supervision, they can be extremely helpful in dieting as appetite suppressants and in the management of severe types of mental illness. However, self-administration of any of the amphetamines—which include benzedrine, dexedrine, methedrine, desbutal, desoxyn, and dexamyl—creates a psychic dependence. An overdose can increase heart action, dangerously elevate blood pressure, and sometimes kill the user. Athletes who depend on these stimulants to increase their endurance during contests requiring prolonged physical exertion sometimes suffer fatal heart attacks. Long-haul truckdrivers who resort to "speed" to stay awake may suffer serious errors in judgment and become involved in dangerous accidents. Sustained wakefulness over a prolonged period of time is extremely harmful. It creates a dangerous dependence on the drug and may produce in some individuals psychosis, hallucinations, and in extreme cases, paranoid delusions. Marked fatigue and lethargy may also be present.

One symptom to be watchful for when you suspect the use of amphetamines is a constant moistening of the mouth. A decrease in saliva causes the lips of the speed or bennie addict to chap and bleed. There will also be apparent a loss of appetite and weight; chronic insomnia, restlessness, irritability, combativeness; profuse perspiration and frequently a resulting strong body odor; a pronounced tremor of the hands; and an elevation in the heartbeat and blood pressure. Overdosage may sometimes cause severe chills, complete collapse, and loss of consciousness. Withdrawal, unless undertaken under skilled medical management, may result in severe depression and attempts at suicide.

The glue sniffer

Glue sniffing is often referred to by users as "flashing." The usual practice is to place some glue in a paper bag and inhale the fumes, which induce a state of euphoria followed by hallucinations. Unfortunately, too many youngsters of high-school age participate in glue flashing for so-called kicks with fatal results. Brain, liver, and kidney damage may occur if the user continues his habit. The glue sniffer's eyes and nose frequently are red and watery. His speech is usually slurred and he staggers from lack of proper coordination. He may appear dazed and collapse in a stupor.

The cocaine user

Pure cocaine, a white, crystal-like powder, is an alkaloid stimulant made from the leaves of the cocoa bush that grows in Bolivia, Java, and Peru. The cocaine user may have a sharp, sweet odor about him. The powder is taken by sniffing through the nose or by injection. The sniffer has raw, red nostrils and a running nose, and the effects are the same whether this substance is sniffed or injected. Prolonged injections of cocaine often cause painful skin abscesses. Other apparent symptoms are loss of appetite and weight, anemia, malnutrition, digestive upsets, convulsions, and paranoid delusions. Drastic mental changes sometimes incite the user to violent physical acts.

The heroin habit

You can usually detect the heroin addict by pronounced changes in the individual's life-style. Heroin causes a temporary state of euphoria that may last for minutes or for hours, depending upon the user's tolerance to this dangerous drug. The addict will usually suffer from malnutrition due to a drastic loss in weight. His complexion will frequently be pasty and covered with sores because he lacks a properly balanced diet. The user's hands and feet are often marked by "needle tracks," and often the individual shows a desire to wear only long-sleeved garments in an effort to hide the marks.

Hepatitis, a serious liver infection that sometimes proves fatal, often attacks addicts when they use unclean needles. Now, still another danger has arisen and threatens to become extremely serious to even non-heroin users unless checked. Recently public health officials detected in the blood of some heroin addicts home from service in Vietnam and elsewhere in Southeast Asia, a virulent, fulminating form of malaria caused by a parasite. Heroin addicts often attempt to sell their blood to commercial transfusion centers to obtain money for a fix. The blood donated by an addict who has been infected or used a dirty needle from a heroin addict with malaria transmits this disease to the patient receiving the transfusion.

Unfortunately, until very recently physicians in the United States were unaware of this danger and unable to diagnose this deadly type of malaria. Early detection and treatment are essential or the outcome may be fatal. Several nonaddict patients in this country became infected with hepatitis and the deadly malaria caused by heroin users' unclean needles, when the blood sold by returned soldier addicts was distributed in several states before detection of the disease. Fortunately, however, in this instance all the patients recovered.

Heroin users often suffer from serious respiratory infections as the result of the suppression of their cough reflexes. Lethargy is another indication of scag addicts, and they seem to have an intense desire for such sweets as soft drinks, candies, and cookies as well as such fresh fruits as mangoes, pineapple, papayas, and bananas, relishing these while refusing other foods.

The "acid head"

Acid heads are users of LSD-25, d-lysergic acid diethylamide tartrate 25, a hallucinogenic semi-synthetic alkaloid obtained from the rye-fungus ergot and the most potent of the hallucinogens. The powder is colorless, odorless, and crystalline, which makes it extremely difficult to detect and very dangerous, since it may be administered in food or drink without the victim's awareness of its presence until hallucinations occur.

The effects vary with the individual. However, they are almost always mind-shattering and users on a "trip" frequently request a "guide" to remain with them and keep them from committing bizarre acts or dangerous attempts at self-destruction. This drug is so mind-distorting that the "acid freak" left alone may attempt to fly out the window or attack anyone within reach. Often violent crimes are committed by users under its influence.

There is no known antidote at this time to the dangerous effects of LSD and often the user will react adversely to a dosage taken a year or more before. Some medical experts believe that prolonged use will cause permanent brain damage as well as chromosome changes that will affect children born to LSD addicts even after use of the drug terminates.

Symptoms include complete personality changes that often turn a well-mannered individual into a crude, shouting irresponsible manic. The acid tripper usually wears dark glasses at all hours, indoors and out, to avoid light, which is extremely painful to his dilated pupils. The eyes of hallucinogenic drug users are usually supersensitive and tear frequently.

The mind distorters

Mescaline, peyote, psilocybin, and psilocin are other mind-distorting hallucinogenic drugs that usually afflict their users with similar symptoms.

Again, we must emphasize the importance of remembering that the drug user is an extremely ill individual who must be treated immediately; and that this is not the time for placing blame, ignoring the unpleasant facts of the critical situation, or having temper tantrums. The foremost objective, we repeat, is to develop communication, empathy, and confidence. You must establish that necessary bridge of trust and understanding that will enable you to immediately summon the expert help that will guide the confused addict out of the drug jungle and back to the world of reality.

CHAPTER III

CROSSING THE BRIDGE:

The Way to Communication and Help

● ● ● ●

The trauma of withdrawal . . . How you can best
communicate . . . If you fail . . . Karen's story . . .
Around-the-clock help . . . The live-in center
Making it clean for keeps . . .

The dangers and critical problems of drug addiction
must be completely understood in order to be effectively treated and alleviated. All too often, I hear the
drug victim painfully disclose that he or she is either
treated as an outcast or completely ignored by family
and friends.

"My folks never talk to me at home," Barbara tear-
fully complained in my office. "I'm trying to get clean
because my friends are not using the stuff any more,
not because my family cares what happens to me. They
never ask what turned me on. All they do is make big
scenes and feel sorry for themselves. I want understanding instead of their ack-ack of insults. I come
home expecting love and encouragement. All I get is a
verbal barrage. If not for my friends watching to make
sure that I don't mainline, I'd shoot the stuff just to
escape from my family!"

39

The trauma of withdrawal

Addicts undergo a period of crisis as severe as in any critical illness the moment their withdrawal from drugs begins. Emotionally, physically, psychologically, and socially, the individual is changing his or her entire life pattern. This severance of all associations with pusher friends and drug users has a traumatic effect on mind and body. It requires sustained determination and will power to remain off the stuff while their junky "friends" are attempting by every possible means to "turn the addict on," even giving "free bags" for fixes so that he or she won't make it clean.

Therefore, at this time you must make every effort to break through any barrier of misunderstanding and gain communication with the drug user. Listen to what he or she wants to say. Don't scold, threaten to punish, or ignore the addict. Remember, this individual is suffering from a grave—often fatal—illness. He needs you to render the help he will need on the long road back.

It is vital when dealing with a drug user that you make the addict aware of your real concern and dedication to help him escape from his or her never-ending nightmare of beanies, junk, acid, or speed. However— and this is absolutely necessary—you must gain the *complete* confidence and trust of the addict to the point where he will cooperate and successfully break the habit.

Unfortunately, as individuals become addicted to drugs, they seem to undergo serious character changes. Promises are broken; they lie and seem to take a delight in cheating members of "straight" society as well as one another. The only thing that appears to matter is mainlining the next fix or planning the next acid trip. All ideas of truthfulness, achievement, and reliability seem to have vanished; they become uptight, nervous, and extremely depressed when off drugs. Often, they sink into a stuporous lethargy and though physically in this world are not part of it. If and when aroused, they become extremely quarrelsome and unable to reason or cope with any situation that requires concentration.

How you can best communicate

What can you do when the drug user refuses or is unable to discuss her or his problem? You must not under any circumstances lose control of the situation. Remember you can summon skillful assistance trained in the management of drug-addiction treatment and withdrawal. Remain calm, cope with the situation, and obtain the essential assistance of experts as soon as possible.

All too frequently, the drug user absolutely refuses to discuss under any circumstances his or her addiction with family or friends. There are several reasons for this reluctance. Many addicts, for one thing, will not admit even to themselves that they are addicted. They prefer to believe that they can take or leave the use of horse, speed, or acid whenever they please. They delude themselves into believing that they are not dependent on dangerous drugs. Some, realizing that they are enslaved by narcotics, are ashamed of themselves and will go to almost any lengths to hide these facts from their families. A frank discussion of the situation with

41

their parents would be shattering to their egos and is therefore to be avoided. Still others are painfully aware of having become drug addicts, yet refuse to discuss the matter for fear of losing their "stuff," plus enduring family anger. And there are addicts who really don't care one way or another, just as long as they have smack for their next fix or acid for the next freak-out.

If you fail

How does one reason with anyone under these circumstances?

Usually it is impossible! Experts often find it extremely difficult to cope with these situations. As discussed in earlier chapters of this book, the family or friends of an addict cannot manage the difficult drug-withdrawal phase alone. The drug user's physical and emotional problems must be handled by experts who work as a team.

Ex-addicts who have successfully kicked the habit have proven to be the best able to communicate since they speak the street language that drug users understand and respect. It has been found in most cases that they make excellent counselors in the withdrawal treatment and long-range therapy programs of hard-drug users. These people, who have experienced the tortures of addiction, are almost always dedicated to helping others escape from a miserable dependence on narcotics. They will spend hours helping a drug user through the agonies of withdrawal or a bad acid trip.

An ex-addict remembers well how when he struggled to kick the habit his physical, as well as emotional, being was almost torn apart through actual pain and mental anguish. If individuals who believe that drugs are something they can take or leave after a few kicks were to witness the withdrawal agonies of a junkie, the hard-drug problem would soon vanish.

Ex-addicts, knowing this, render invaluable assistance during the actual withdrawal phase as well as in the long counseling and therapy programs. Therefore, it is absolutely necessary that communication be established with the drug user by someone of his or her age group who has already been there, and can "tell it as it is" to the addict who refuses to discuss the problem with family, parents, or friends.

Once communication has been established—even if only on a limited basis—it is a start in the right direction. It makes possible the essential contact with the drug user. Now the counselor can reach out and, in the language of the drug culture, speak to the addict in need of help.

Karen's story

Recently, Karen, a seventeen-year-old high-school senior, who had started smoking pot at fourteen and then went on to mainline heroin, told me in my office after she started the methadone treatment: "You know, doctor, if only my parents would have listened to me when I wanted to talk to them three years ago when I started smoking reefers. They just refused to admit to themselves that I, who seemingly had all the advantages, could possibly be on drugs. When they found out, do you think they cared? They were uptight about what their friends and neighbors would say. That's the trouble, they never thought about me. Sure, they gave me the good things—nice clothes, a big pad, and a new car. They never cared that I was lonely and didn't have anyone to talk to, or relate what was happening with drugs at school. The kids were all getting high. I wanted to belong, and the only way I could was to become part of the drug scene. We started with pot and went on to junk. You know," Karen further confided, "I guess I still wouldn't try to kick it. One reason is, I like to see my folks squirm and be ashamed of me, but my friends are on this program to stop using heroin, and if they are kicking the habit, that's the thing to do! They decided to try and do something useful with their lives, and I want to do the same!"

Karen poignantly makes clear how much the success or failure of the treatment depends on the continued understanding and encouragement of those close to and important to the life-style of the drug user.

Around-the-clock help

The addict is sensitive, unsure, and undergoing severe physical and emotional stress. That is why it is so important that the patient be counseled by and attend meetings of his or her peer group who have successfully broken the drug habit or are in the process of so doing. You can now obtain the names and phone numbers of counselors available around-the-clock so that you can reach them in case of an emergency. This will not only give you confidence in the management of any situation that develops, but will also show the drug addict how much you really care and want him to make it clean.

44

Awareness House, of which I am staff medical adviser, was opened in Tucson, Arizona, in October, 1969. It was created as a community cost-free effort designed to prevent and stop drug abuse among youngsters in the area. Closeness to the Mexican border at Nogales poses a special problem for the law-enforcement authorities of both countries. Despite strict inspection of suspected drug smugglers, the stuff is comparatively simple to obtain in this area, according to the addicts. Youngsters, of junior and senior high-school age, as well as college students and "street people," are subject to constant temptation if their associates are addicts. All too often, a youngster unknowingly becomes addicted to drugs due to the zealous dope pusher's "missionary" efforts. This so-called friend is usually a school classmate who is eager to share this deadly delight with his or her pal!

Awareness House is one of several such programs established in major cities throughout the United States—New York, Los Angeles, and San Francisco among them. More are in the planning stage. (See page 145 for locations in your area.) Youngsters withdrawing from drugs need to form new, healthy friendships and meet other individuals like themselves who have experienced the same narcotic habits, and who have successfully broken away from their old life-style and become clean. I send my patients to Awareness House for the excellent counseling it makes available to them in the communications groups, and for the opportunities it offers to acquire new meaningful values and interests.

Sandra, a pert and pretty patient of mine, is eighteen.

A former five-trip-a-day drug user, she is now a coed at the university. She is on the methadone treatment. During a recent office visit, she said, "Doctor, I come over to Awareness House all the time. It's a great place. Sometimes I find myself being tempted with the stuff. When I start daydreaming about smack, I know I can level with one of the counselors. We can communicate because they know what it is like—they kicked the habit and know how tough it is sometimes to stay clean. They straighten out my thinking real fast. This is my life line back to the real world that I very much need. I know I can always depend on the counselors at Awareness House to be available whenever I need them!"

When an addict comes to my office and says, "Please help me, Doctor, I want to kick the habit," I know that if the patient is sincerely willing to cooperate and work with me on the long, difficult road back, fortunately there are available at Awareness House dedicated young counselors whose personal experience enables them to communicate with the addict. I count on them to get the message across that drugs are deadly and that slavish day-to-day dependence can be stopped.

The live-in center

We must have live-in and counseling centers for drug users, for they need a strictly controlled environment. They must be shielded from all temptation while undergoing withdrawal treatment until they develop sufficient will power to resist the efforts of their former associates to lure them back to that living death. They require proper medical attention, professional counsel-

46

ing, rehabilitation on all levels, and the establishment of a new way of life. They must be made aware that they have a real contribution to make to society, and that they are very important to themselves and their families.

When it is necessary to create interest, they can at a live-in center be taught creative arts and crafts and other forms of meaningful self-expression. Tucson's Awareness House teaches the almost-forgotten arts of candlemaking and leatherworking. The youngsters can feel the pride of achievement by contributing creative crafts to society while at the same time they are helping to sustain themselves financially.

This combined therapy of counseling, creative work, and medical treatment has been extremely successful. A live-in center is essential to the successful treatment of drug users. If contributions make it impossible to confine the addict to such a treatment center, then several hours a week of counseling must be scheduled.

Making it clean for keeps

All too often, medical therapy alone is inadequate. Temptation abounds and it is far too easy for the addict to slip back into his or her past environment. There must be a complete and final break with all junkie associates. Far too frequently, one hears young patients say, "Doctor, I really tried." Paul, a once-handsome seventeen-year-old high-school track star, is typical of this unfortunate pattern. "I just couldn't stay away from the kids," he told me. "I was lonely and didn't have anyone to talk to nor any place to go!"

Unless a complete break is made with the user's drug

environment, tragic consequences may result, despite any well-intentioned wish to kick the habit the addict may express. The following is an excerpt of a letter sent to me by the mother of a brilliant high-school student who was unable to sever his connections with the drug scene.

March 11, 1970

Dear Dr. Alexander:

I want to thank you for all the help you have given my son, Robert.

The words of encouragement that you gave him during the visits to your office and the methadone helped greatly and did more for him than anything else.

Unfortunately, he couldn't stay away from the drug pushers. He is now in County Jail awaiting transfer to a youth camp for sixty days' observation. Robert will undergo careful evaluation during this time by court-appointed medical and probation experts. If he does well within this time, he may get probation or a sentence of from six to eighteen months in a youth camp.

During the next two months, if he can't make it without drugs the court will change the present charge, possession of heroin, to a felony and place him in a prison hospital.

I sincerely believe that when Robert is completely removed from the drug-scene associations here that have plagued him, he will be able to live a normal, productive life without heroin.

His confinement to a small jail cell is extremely difficult and a nerve-racking experience for him now, as he awaits word about the judge's decision and his future hangs in the balance.

Thank you again and again for all of your help and continued efforts on behalf of Robert and the many other young addicts. You are their hope in this pretty mixed-up scene.

Sincerely,
Mrs. A. S.

The letter illustrates a very tragic situation that happens all too often. Youngsters, try as they will, usually cannot break the habit of dangerous drug usage alone. The treatment must be continued for months afterward if they are going to firmly establish a new, healthy life-style away from the drug-pusher scene. Unfortunately, like Paul, some addicts return to drugs shortly after withdrawal simply because they do not receive the essential continuing treatment of counseling and communication. Awareness House's communication groups meet at least twice a week for three hours or more at a time. And if an individual develops sudden seemingly overwhelming desire for the stuff, counselors are immediately available to handle the situation.

Kathy, a sixteen-year-old patient and former four-trip-a-day user of scag, told me: "I come to Awareness House all the time just to make sure I won't use junk again. When I find myself daydreaming about the stuff, I know I can talk to the counselors. They make me see things as they are. They know what it's like. I clean up my thinking fast. They do a great job in straightening out us kids!"

CHAPTER IV

BACK TO REALITY:

Is Methadone the Way?

● ● ● ●

How it works . . . Is it addictive? . . . What are the alternatives? . . . Washington progress report . . . Hope for New York City's 100,000 addicts . . . Prognosis . . .

There is no special formula guaranteed to cure all the various types of drug addiction. Treatment that may prove helpful to one individual may not have any beneficial effect on another. However, I have found in my practice that the methadone maintenance program produces excellent results. Approximately 80 percent of those receiving the drug under proper, constant medical supervision are able to kick the heroin habit in a period of time ranging from months to a year or two.

How it works

Methadone (4, 4-diphenyl-6-dimethylamino-3-hepta-none) is a synthetic opiate analgesic. This drug was synthesized by German chemists prior to World War II and came into use in the United States in the late nine-teen-forties. The methadone treatment replaces addiction to heroin in that treatment with this medication generally suppresses the desire for heroin and its euphoria. The purpose is to enable the addict to withdraw from heroin and break away from his or her life-style of drugs under close medical supervision. Dolophine tablets are usually prescribed; the addicts frequently refer to these as "dollies." Daily dosage may vary from 100 to 180 milligrams, which is taken orally with orange juice. Methadone occasionally creates an unpleasant but not undesirable effect if the heroin addict attempts to backslide and use both together. Once the addict becomes adjusted to the methadone maintenance program, he or she has no further need for heroin since it is no longer a means of reaching a temporary state of euphoria.

Is it addictive?

The methadone treatment was first successfully pioneered by Doctors Vincent Dole and Marie Nyswander in 1964 in New York City. This treatment is not without its side effects, for some patients develop a dependence on methadone. However, the relatively small percentage of individuals who may become addicted to methadone are able to live a normal life. They can successfully hold jobs and make a useful contribution to society instead of remaining hopelessly addicted to heroin and unable to care for themselves. Some of my patients who formerly mainlined four or five times a day are now employed in the copper mines of Southern Arizona, where the work is rugged and requires excellent physical health. Joe, a native of California who came to Arizona to escape the drug scene of his buddies, has this to say about it: "Doctor, I never felt better in my life since taking methadone. I feel great working in the mines. Now, for the first time, I know I am accomplishing something worthwhile!"

What are the alternatives?

Two new drugs now being tested are believed to be nonaddictive and hold promise of freeing addicts from their dependence on heroin or a substitute such as methadone. Doctors Alfred M. Freedman and Max Fink, prominent New York City physicians specializing in psychiatry and neurology, describe the drugs cyclazocine and nalaxone as opiate antagonists that block the action of heroin so that an individual has no more response to the drug than if he received an injection of salt water.

Addicts would require three injections of cyclazocine a week or one dose of nalaxone a day. Doctors Freedman and Fink believe that the drugs may eventually be used to immunize persons—service personnel, for example—against addiction. These drugs are now being tested in several major cities in the United States. However, a serious obstacle that prevents the mass manufacture of nalaxone is that this drug is obtained from an opium derivative that cannot be legally imported into this country.

Washington progress report

Drug usage, we know, is a form of rebellion or escape from the realities and responsibilities of daily life and its decision making. The drug user must be made aware that copping out will not alleviate the dissatisfactions that have alienated him from life. Only by facing his problems will he be able to change matters. This means kicking the drug habit. This understanding on the part of the addict is essential in order to begin effective withdrawal treatment.

It shows in the record. Authorities point out that as drug addiction increases throughout the country the crime rate soars. Illegal drug traffic in the Washington area, according to a recent report to Congress, states that the combination of increased police emphasis on illegal narcotics and methadone-treatment procedures are credited for the drop in drug usage and crime in the District of Columbia.

The use of illegal drugs in the Washington area and its Maryland and Virginia suburbs costs residents and businesses 250 million dollars annually in robberies, shoplifting, burglaries, and other crimes by addicts. There are approximately ten thousand heroin addicts in the Washington area. It is estimated that on the average each of them steals and panhandles $458 a week to support the drug habit! According to the report, "The law-enforcement efforts against narcotics dealers have been effective enough so that ex-addict pushers now characterize the streets of the national capital as 'hot' for drug pushers."

The report particularly praises the Narcotics Treatment Administration, calling it the "first comprehensive, citywide narcotics-treatment program in the nation." The Narcotics Treatment Administration (NTA) uses methadone, administering it daily to heroin addicts. The NTA is currently treating about twenty-two hundred addicts at a cost of about one thousand dollars a year for each patient. The officials in charge of the Narcotics Treatment Administration in the District of Columbia find that this program is extremely worthwhile to the addicts as well as to the community. The crime rate has dropped because more drug users are now self-sufficient instead of burdens to the taxpayers and themselves.

Hope for New York City's 100,000 addicts

After a period of several years of evaluating the beneficial results of methadone as opposed to its side effects, New York City officials have announced plans to quadruple the city's maintenance-treatment program. The city has requested $9,200,000 from New York Governor Nelson A. Rockefeller to provide methadone-dispensing programs throughout the city.

The plan includes distribution by private physicians on a test basis instead of limiting it to clinics and hospitals. Governor Rockefeller's projected 1971-72 budget has requested 24 million dollars from the New York State Legislature for methadone programs throughout the state that will meet its desperate need for addict withdrawal therapy.

Mayor John V. Lindsay has stated that the $9,200,000 would prove to be "an essential investment to reduce the hundreds of millions of dollars in crimes that now result from addicts' addiction to heroin."

The city's current methadone program, which is administered through health clinics or hospitals, has five hundred patients under treatment with an anticipated total of twenty-five hundred in a few months. During the first three months of operation, more than that number of requests for treatment had been received. Applications are being processed at the rate of over three hundred weekly, and twelve of the twenty-two planned treatment units are now open.

According to New York State's figures, there are now more than one hundred thousand addicts in New York City alone! The seven thousand now on the methadone program are but a small fraction of those addicts without treatment who are still living desperately and without hope.

Careful evaluation of the methadone-treatment programs conducted in New York City at Beth Israel Hospital and at the Columbia University School of Public Health and Administrative Medicine disclose that patients who remain in the program on methadone therapy—and more than 80 percent do—are off heroin, while a few use it infrequently.

After a period of two years, 75 percent of the patients on the program are employed or in school and are self-sustaining members of society. Only 20 percent require welfare or some other means of assistance. There is an arrest rate of only 5 percent; the remaining 95 percent are not in any difficulty with the law.

Prognosis

We cannot expect methadone or any other drug to be an instant or permanent cure-all for all the problems resulting from heroin addiction. However, in a great many cases it has enabled addicts to embark on carefully supervised medical psychotherapy programs and take the first necessary measures to become useful, productive members of society. A New York City med-

55

ical social worker discussing the proposed $9,200,000 increase in the methadone program made the following comment: "Methadone helps get addicts off the streets. Look around and you'll see how important it is to get these junkies off the streets before they destroy the city and themselves!"

CHAPTER V

THE RIGHT DIET:

What It Can Do for the Addict

• • • •

Double jeopardy, starvation and drug poisoning . . . When hospitalization is necessary . . . The high-caloric liquids and snacks . . . What exercises to do . . . The first signs of recovery . . . A diet plan you can follow at home . . . The liquid diet and sample menu . . . The soft diet and sample menu . . . The high-caloric semi-fluid diet and sample menu . . . The high-caloric diet and sample menu . . .

Patients being treated for prolonged narcotic usage always suffer from serious malnutrition. Many drug addicts being treated for withdrawal are in such critical condition from starvation that they must be fed intravenously with glucose and vitamins if they are to survive.

Double jeopardy, starvation and drug poisoning

Unfortunately, some hard-drug users are in such a deteriorated mental state that they neglect the nutritional requirements necessary for survival. They are completely unaware that they are subjecting themselves to the double jeopardy of death by starvation as well as drug poisoning. Until recently, most physicians in the United States (except those in the poverty areas) did not see many cases of critical malnutrition among teen-agers and adults. When isolated cases were observed, the causes were pathological or mental problems in mature adults, or the inability of some very young children to digest food.

However, as the drug plague has increased to epidemic levels, many of the young adults who come in for withdrawal therapy must at the same time be treated for malnutrition. The sadness of this situation is that these people are starving and do not even know that they are hungry!

A drug such as heroin suppresses all normal body wants, including the desire for food. Thus, while the addict may be spending one hundred dollars or more a day for fixes, he or she may be starving to death. Addicts frequently suffer from recurring attacks of nausea and vomiting caused by lack of food. Often, when they become vaguely aware of agonizing hunger pangs, they develop an abnormal craving for sweets with high sugar content such as candy, cakes, and soft drinks. As mentioned earlier, one of the discernible indications of heroin use is the desire for sweets to the exclusion of all other foods. However, as we know, this does not supply sufficient nourishment to the diet. If malnutrition continues over a prolonged period of time without expert medical treatment, death may result from starvation.

When hospitalization is necessary

A nutritious diet, therefore, is an extremely important part of the therapy in drug-withdrawal treatment. Occasionally, to save the drug abuser's life, we must order immediate hospitalization for addiction and starvation. Intravenous feedings are given to supply the critically needed nourishment to the victim's weakened body and to restore the proper balance of proteins, vitamins, and fluids. The intravenous administration of glucose and vitamins assists the liver, restores circulation, aids the other organs to function properly, and at the same time creates a desire and tolerance for food. A victim of starvation cannot eat or digest solid food, so the patient is encouraged at this time to take orally, if possible, ginger ale and such fruit juices as papaya and orange.

The high caloric liquids and snacks

Gradually, as the individual responds to treatment, the liquid diet may be increased to supply the essential nutrients in fluid form. This consists of bland but appetizing foods such as cream soups, soft-boiled eggs, strained fruits and vegetables, milk, gelatin puddings, custards, ice cream, and tapioca. Between-meal snacks of fruit juices, milk, eggnogs, and crackers are encouraged. (See sample menus at end of chapter.)

We must remember that the patient on withdrawal treatment must be encouraged to eat a high-caloric, nourishing diet in order to strengthen a body that is suffering from serious vitamin, mineral, and protein deficiencies. The mental outlook and mood of the individual becomes increasingly optimistic and cooperative as his or her physical condition improves. A normal desire for food usually indicates that the patient is now on the road to recovery.

What exercises to do

Care, however, must be taken to insure that this improvement is maintained and that the individual receives sufficient exercise, too. A gradually increasing program of exercise will restore muscle tone to the body, which undoubtedly has broken down due to disuse, weakness, and malnutrition.

I encourage my patients to exercise as soon as they have sufficient strength. The program starts with walking a short distance and then gradually, as the physical condition permits, increasing activity to include swimming, baseball, basketball, and other forms of exercise both indoors and outdoors. Of course, whenever possible I prefer that the patient exercise in the fresh air. The combination of a well-balanced attractive diet and an exercise program proves extremely beneficial to the addict who is being treated for heroin abuse with methadone.

The first signs of recovery

The patient is almost always undergoing tremendous tension and pressure from peer groups on both sides. His pusher friends are urging that the victim return to the enslavement of the drug scene while his family, his friends who have successfully kicked the habit, and his counselors are encouraging the addict to "stay with the program" and get "clean." All too often the drug user is thoroughly confused and tottering on the brink of complete mental and physical collapse under the pressure of indecision. However, when he or she notices a renewed interest in food, an improved complexion, a return of physical strength, and a re-awakened desire for sex, the patient will cooperate completely to expedite narcotic withdrawal. Usually, from this point on, the patient becomes less difficult and more likely to succeed.

Diet and exercise—in addition to building the patient's strength and renewing interest in his or her surroundings—also serve to widen his horizon of helpful friends and healthful atmosphere with new things to learn and accomplish. Meanwhile he gains more and more confidence in his own ability to kick the habit and stay clean.

It is at this time that the addict on withdrawal treatment requires of all those interested in his or her recovery the most patient and tactful counseling. As stated earlier in this chapter, the slightest change in the program may turn the patient against withdrawal therapy and send him back to the drug world. The drug user is extremely sensitive and often fancies slights that do not exist.

Time and again I have noted that once the patient realizes the importance of food to his or her good health, he expresses an immediate interest in learning what else can be done to help him remove the toxic drugs still plaguing his body. Unfortunately, some hard drugs and their toxic effects create long-term problems.

Glue sniffers, for example, can inflict irreversible damage to their livers; the results are sometimes fatal.

Again, I wish to stress in the strongest possible terms that once permanent damage has been caused by the use of drugs, neither therapy nor diet nor exercise will reverse the downward course. Fortunately, however, as more drug users become aware of the dangers of narcotics and willingly seek help to rid themselves of this vice, it is hoped that they kick the habit before their minds and bodies are damaged permanently.

A diet plan you can follow at home

Make no mistake about it—in the beginning it may be extremely difficult to interest in food, the patient undergoing withdrawal therapy, but on the following pages you will find lists of nourishing foods that can be temptingly prepared. We have included their nutrient values and the reasons for selecting these menus in relation to the various phases of patients' tolerances. We start with the liquid diet and gradually increase it to the soft, bland foods, and finally, as they can be tolerated and required by the individual (needs differ with the patient), the normal or high-caloric diets.

The most nutritious diets are those that include foods with proteins, carbohydrates, fats, minerals, salts, sugar, vitamins, and water. These are all essential to the human body. Proteins, carbohydrates, and fats are sources of energy The individual's requirements are best determined by the physician after a careful examination of the patient. Patients suffering from severe loss of weight from illness or drug addiction will be placed on a high-caloric diet; those wishing to lose excess poundage will be advised to follow a low-caloric plan. However, every diet, whether low or high in calories, must have all the essential nutrients and basic foods vital to the establishment and maintenance of the individual's good health. Menus must be planned to be attractive, with a sufficient variety of foods to be interesting and make dining a pleasure instead of a bothersome chore.

The following suggested diets have been carefully selected to provide guidelines to the essential nutrients. You will find all basic food groups—eggs, fish, meats, fruits, vegetables, fats and oils, milk and milk products, cereals and whole-grain breads. A carefully balanced menu is extremely important, whether the program is a high- or low-caloric one.

The liquid diet and sample menu

When a liquid diet is indicated, more protein may be included by adding gelatin, whole egg, casein, powdered milk, and protein hydrolysates to the liquids in the diet.

The best method of preparing a liquid diet is to place the food in a blender and leave it in the container attached to the machine until it is liquefied. Any food that is not difficult to digest usually lends itself to blending. Custard, jello, puddings, ice cream, and poached or soft-boiled eggs can be included in the liquid diet if tolerated by the patient.

It may be necessary at first to schedule frequent small feedings instead of the usual three meals daily to gradually accustom the individual to food.

SAMPLE MENU
LIQUID DIET

Breakfast	*Lunch*	*Dinner*
Fruit juice, 6 oz.— orange, papaya, tomato, apricot, strawberry, or pear	Fruit juice, 6 oz. Cream soup Custard or jello Strained fruit Milk or milkshake, 8 oz.	Fruit juice, 6 oz. Cream soup Two strained vegetables Pudding or gelatin Milk or malted, 8 oz.
Strained cereal, with milk and sugar		
Poached or soft egg		
Milk or eggnog		

Any of the above foods can be taken as between-meal snacks and at bedtime, as tolerated.

The soft diet and sample menu

A soft diet is indicated when, due to weakness or a gastrointestinal condition, the individual is unable to digest normal foods. This provides essential nourishment that is easily digested. The menu consists of the following foods:

Cereals (fine wheat)
Bread (enriched or white)
Banana
Cooked fruits (without seeds or skin)
Eggs
Cheese
Custards
Cake (sponge and angel food)
Fish
Fowl

Finely ground beef

Gelatin (jello)

Milk

Potatoes

Rice

All fried foods are to be avoided. Other items that should be excluded from the soft diet are: coarse cereals, strong spices, pork, veal, raw fruits and vegetables, and all rich desserts. Prepare fish and meat by broiling, baking, or poaching.

SAMPLE MENU
SOFT DIET

Breakfast	Lunch	Dinner
Fruit juice, 6 oz.	Cream soup	3 oz. fish, fowl, or
½ cup whole-wheat	2 oz. fish or	ground meat
or enriched cereal	ground beef	Potatoes or rice
with milk and	Rice, noodles,	1 slice bread and
sugar	or potatoes	butter
Poached or soft-	2 strained	2 strained
boiled egg	vegetables	vegetables
1 slice bread and	1 slice bread and	Dessert—select from
butter	butter	puddings, custard,
Milk or tea	Ripe banana,	cake, or jello
	custard, or jello	Milk, 8 oz.
	milk, 8 oz.	

Any of these foods are interchangeable and may be used according to individual taste as long as the diet is followed. For instance, if the patient prefers noodles at both lunch and dinner, this is permitted as long as the food is tolerated and the necessary amount of calories are included in the daily menu.

The high-caloric semi-fluid diet and sample menu

The principle of this diet is to provide nourishing food that the patient can tolerate. The individual is encouraged to have frequent small feedings whenever desired.

SAMPLE MENU
HIGH-CALORIC SEMI-FLUID DIET

Breakfast	Lunch	Dinner
Fruit juice with sugar added	Cream soup	Chicken or beef broth
Fine cereal with cream and sugar	Cheese	Cheese or egg
Egg (poached or soft-boiled)	Noodles	Baked potato with butter
Bread, butter, and jam	1 slice bread and butter	1 slice bread and butter
Milk, 8 oz.	Milk, 8 oz.	Custard, jello, or ice cream
		Milk, 8 oz.

Midmorning	Midafternoon	Bedtime
Milk 6 oz. with 10 per cent or more cream plus several crackers	Fruit juice enriched with sugar	Eggnog or milkshake
		Crackers, if desired

The high-caloric diet and sample menu

This diet is indicated when the individual is suffering from malnutrition. The normal diet is supplemented with foods rich in calories such as butter, cream, avocados, bananas, butter, cakes, cream cheese, dried fruits, gelatin desserts, honey, ice cream, jams, jellies, whole milk, nuts (as tolerated), sugar, sweetened soft drinks, syrups, eggnog, and gravies. Care, however,

66

must be taken that too much rich food does not upset the individual's digestion; it should be added to the menu only as tolerated.

SAMPLE MENU
HIGH CALORIC DIET

Breakfast	*Lunch*	*Dinner*
Fruit juice, 8 oz., with added sugar	Cream soup	3 oz. fish, fowl, or meat
Cereal with cream and sugar	2 oz. meat, fish, or cheese	Vegetable with cream sauce
1 or 2 eggs	Vegetable with butter sauce	Noodles or rice
2 slices enriched bread, butter, honey or jam	Noodles, rice, or potatoes	Salad with dressing
Milk or coffee, or tea with cream and sugar	2 slices bread and butter	2 slices bread and butter
	Fruit or dessert such as jello or custard	Rich dessert
	Milk, 8 oz.	Milk, 8 oz., 10 to 20 percent cream

Midmorning, midafternoon, and night-time snacks as desired. This should include milk, eggnog, cake, and crackers.

Recent research has shown that, when the organs of the body are deprived of nutrients that include proteins with the essential amino acids, carbohydrates, fats, and vitamins, the individual will suffer from chronic fatigue and mental depression. Sugar is a source of energy for the brain, and proteins and vitamins provide the body muscles and tissues with the necessary nutrients to function normally. The addict coming off drugs must be made to understand that sound principles of nutrition must be followed in conjunction with withdrawal therapy in order to expedite treatment.

I have found that most of my patients are eager to cooperate in planning nutritious diets to help them overcome the ravages of self-inflicted starvation while under the influence of hard drugs. They usually find it challenging and interesting to plan their own high-caloric menus, which contain, incidentally, more than the twenty-four hundred to three thousand calories per day recommended for men's normal daily diet and the two thousand to twenty-four hundred for women. Calories are increased or decreased to meet specific requirements.

They moreover find it extremely satisfying to plan menus wherein calories don't count! Some good sources of protein such as abalone, oysters, and eggs are reputed to have aphrodisiac qualities and are extremely popular items on the diet lists. As I discussed earlier, once the drug abuser comes off heroin, his sex drive returns. Consequently, since some foods such as those mentioned are believed to enhance sexual drive, they are often scheduled on the menu. There is no scientific basis for this, of course, but it serves the very useful purpose of supplying vital proteins to individuals needing them and certainly adds to the eating pleasure.

CHAPTER VI

TO KEEP YOUR CHILDREN OFF DRUGS:

Permissiveness, Overprotection, or Discipline?

● ● ● ●

The healthy, supportive home life . . . A two-way
communication . . . Don't be conned . . . A change
of environment . . . The community team . . .
Middle-age delinquents . . .

Peter, the eighteen-year-old son of a retired Air Force
officer, decided to kick his heroin habit for several
reasons. Several members of his peer group had
successfully discarded the use of drugs, and his hundred-
dollar-a-day habit was far too expensive for his high-
school allowance. He tried to supplement his finances
by stealing, but could not shoplift enough to support
his craving for heroin.

Peter leveled with his parents and went to see a
physician to end his drug addiction. He was placed on
methadone maintenance therapy and was doing extremely well until his father passed some sarcastic re-
mark about his need for methadone and refused to pay
for the continuance of this medication. The boy, completely confused, took the car and fled to another area.
His whereabouts were discovered when he sought treatment for a self-inflicted wound in the chest that had

become infected. This tragic attempt at self-destruction was an act of desperation brought about by his unsympathetic father's cynical attitude!

Fortunately, Peter recovered from his attempt at suicide, and when his parents brought him home, they realized that he must be encouraged to attend the meetings of youngsters with similar problems at Tucson's Awareness House. These personal encounters with others of his own age made Peter feel less alone, and with additional help from a physician trained in the careful management of such cases, Peter returned to school and kicked the habit.

This is not an isolated case. Drug users who have become clean are unfortunately often driven back to their habits, not by their own failure to break their dependence on narcotics but rather by unsympathetic family feelings. Please remember, when addicts are attempting to withdraw from drugs, they are giving up more than just their habit. The complete life-style of the user is oriented to the world of junkies. It is much simpler for the user of heroin, acid, or speed to return to familiar surroundings and drift back into a state of euphoria than it is to battle the physical and mental anguish that exist when relinquishing the habit.

The healthy, supportive home life

Make no mistake about it! It does require tremendous will power on the part of the individual who has determined to free himself from drug dependence. This effort should be recognized, and the drug user should be commended and encouraged for facing the dangerous situation and striving to correct it with the assistance of skilled medical management.

The family as well as the drug user is under tremendous pressure. The situation requires everyone's determination, patience, and tolerance. I do not believe that sympathy will have any beneficial results. Actually, serious harm may result from too much coddling at this particular time of treatment. Unfortunately, before kicking the habit and becoming clean, the addict will often lie, cheat, and rage to gain sympathy and obtain "bread" to buy junk for the habit that he or she is allegedly attempting to overcome.

However, as in Peter's case, a complete lack of empathy may drive the addict back to the very dangerous life-style that he or she is struggling to escape. Therefore, I urge my patients and their families to have understanding and tolerance for each other. It is extremely important during all phases of treatment, as well as after, to make the drug user feel accepted, wanted, and needed as a member of the family group.

A two-way communication

Let the patient feel that he may at any moment frankly discuss with you his problems, whether they are emotional, financial, physical, or social. Do not demand or insist that questions be answered immediately with a one-word reply of yes or no. This practice is frequently considered an obvious sign of distrust and very much resented. Instead, skillfully and patiently make the individual know that you are really sincerely interested. This is the way to gain the confidence of the drug user.

This is how you will develop the necessary two-way communication that will make possible discussion of the addict's past and present problems.

You must show your concern, interest, and helpfulness without indulging in pity, either for the addict or for yourself. Listen patiently when the patient wants to level with you.

Don't be conned

You must not under any circumstances permit the drug user to con you into believing that, although he is trying to kick the habit, he needs some bread for just one more shot to overcome extreme nervousness. If you detect any fresh needle marks or suspect by the individual's slurred speech, too-bright eyes, extreme sleepiness, or state of euphoria that drugs are again being used, contact immediately the physician in charge of the withdrawal treatment.

Addicts undergoing withdrawal treatment sometimes attempt to delude their families and physicians. When this occurs, only prompt, expert attention will protect the addict from his or her own self-destructive action. Often they think of this as a game, or a challenge to your powers of observation to see if you really care enough.

Terry, a high-school student, stared at his needle-marked, ulcerated hands while seated in my office and remarked: "If only my folks would have listened when I wanted to level with them about the kids at school getting stoned on the stuff. If only they would have been interested enough to tell me not to get hooked, I might never have started shooting horse. My parents never seemed to notice what I did until I got busted by the fuzz. My mother only cared about her bridge tournaments and my father's real hang-up was his golf score! Now, they tell me that they care but I can't even be sure about that!"

Unfortunately, there is no magic formula that makes it possible for the family of the drug user to bridge the enormous gulf that separates the world of reality from the narcotic-oriented scene. It requires patience, constant watchfulness, and cooperation to achieve the de sired goal of complete drug withdrawal.

There will be many instances of stress and tension for everybody concerned. New friends, interests, hobbies, ambitions, and social life must be carefully planned to avoid the very real temptations that can lure the narcotic user, who is attempting to kick the habit, back into his or her former life-style. The many excellent halfway houses throughout the country will help make the addict aware that the straight world is more worthwhile than the crazy, mixed-up scene of Junkies and Acid Heads.

A change in environment

If it is impossible for the addict to escape from the harmful influence of drug users, I insist upon an immediate change of environment. The addict should be sent to a distant area, away from his or her familiar life-style. If this proves impossible, it may be necessary to commit the drug victim to an institution for treatment. The addict, ill emotionally as well as physically, is unable to help himself. You must make all the decisions concerning his welfare, his very existence. If you hesitate or do nothing, you are losing valuable time that may ultimately mean the difference between life and death.

The community team

Since drug addicition has become a serious national problem, families of victims have begun to band together in organizations throughout the country to share experiences and develop means of assisting in withdrawal efforts. They meet at each other's homes or at community centers to discuss the facts of addiction and the value of more positive action toward the improvement of their own, as well as the drug users', shortcomings and environment.

Drug users, however, often deeply resent their families' participation in discussion and self-help groups. They prefer the advice and assistance of their peers.

Terri, a pert brunette college junior, told me: "My mom really digs this Tuesday-night meeting of her group. It gives her the chance to sound off about what a freak I am and how patient and great she is about putting up with her heroin-hooked daughter! I know other kids are just as uptight about their folks doing the same about them. It makes our parents feel important while we're torn apart as monsters.

"Our folks should want to know what turned us on and try to help us instead of yapping about their own special freaks! Sure, we need help. We want to be treated as human beings, not monsters. We feel that our folks get together to talk about how bad we are instead of remembering that they aren't so great, either. They haven't set us such good examples of what is right and wrong. Many a time I've seen my father looped on bourbon and my mom popping tranquilizers into her mouth like candy. Sometimes I would want to talk to her about my schoolwork, but she was always too busy or too tired or going out to a party. They think it's okay for them to do these things and when I turn on with scag they scream. It's not that they really care what happens to me that makes them act up. They are afraid that their friends will find out, and they won't be accepted anymore in their own fun group. They are just as hung up on alcohol and pills as we are, but they won't admit their faults. They blame us for everything!

"Sure, turning on with drugs isn't smart. I know that now. But our folks should set us a better example. It's time they stop tearing us apart and start helping us! This world of theirs needs trust and understanding. When they honestly face up to things as they are and we start communicating with each other, we may be able to work out our differences. However, we need the help and cooperation of our folks to change our environment and life-style."

Middle-age delinquents

Main Street, U.S.A., in the nineteen-seventies—whether it is Westport, Connecticut, or Wenatchee, Washington—has many of the same problems in facing up to the drug plague that is infecting our youth. However, to be absolutely accurate, not all drug abusers are young. There are quite a few individuals in their forties who pop pills and smoke marijuana. However, these groups of middle-age delinquents

75

hold their bennie or pot parties in order to be different and in a futile attempt to recapture their long-past youth rather than because of a real liking for the drugs. Fortunately, these over-age dropouts are a minority, and youthful addicts view them with distrust.

Until recently the drug problem was believed to be confined to such large urban areas as New York, San Francisco, or New Orleans. Now that this epidemic is national in scope, drug pushers pedal their illicit wares in schools and shaded streets of rural areas as frequently as in crowded cities. Youngsters of twelve use and sell heroin in Wenatchee in the same manner as their counterparts in the slums of New York. Buying the stuff is all too easy, whether on the country lane or in the back alley of a city. The quiet town very often has as much of a drug problem as the city ghetto, but too frequently it is permitted to reach epidemic levels before measures are taken to stop its growth.

Many times parents and authorities, especially in these rural areas, have refused to face up to the drug problem in a mistaken belief that ignoring the situation will make it disappear. Now, as they become aware that drug abuse is as much a part of Main Street and rural America as of the crowded city, they are becoming involved in the educational programs of addiction that better enable them to handle these problems effectively. Environment is more than beautiful, tree-shaded streets and green lawns. It is the determination of adults and young people everywhere to work together to create a drug-free atmosphere through education, understanding, and action.

CHAPTER VII

SOME POPULAR MISCONCEPTIONS:

Former Addicts Speak Up

● ● ● ●

The drug prone . . . The underground . . . The
alienated . . . The street people . . .

"I grew pot in my backyard in Hollywood," Steve, a
former five-fix-a-day mainliner, disclosed in a matter-of-
fact manner. Steve is now an extremely dedicated
counselor on the staff of Tucson's Awareness House.
He successfully handles the most difficult narcotic-
withdrawal cases with patience and firmness. Addicts
listen to him with respect. They know he has experienced the same intense craving for hard drugs that they
so painfully endure while undergoing withdrawal
treatment.

There is no better or more reputable missionary in
the drug picture than the former addict who has stayed
clean. They are excellent examples of successful achievement for the addict who sincerely seeks treatment.

"I started smoking joy sticks back in Chicago when I
was fifteen," continued Steve. "I didn't have a particularly happy home life. I guess I would have started
smoking reefers, anyway. Almost everyone I knew at

school was doing it. I came home fogged up half the time. My folks were so busy fighting with each other, they never noticed or cared what happened to me. I left school and took off for California when I was sixteen. There was a lot of action around Haight-Ashbury when I made the San Francisco scene a few years ago. I got hooked on horse there. I had to push the stuff and burn [steal] all the time just to take care of my needs. All I cared about was where and how soon I had my next fix. I was busted so many times by the fuzz that I took off for L.A. A lot of us drifted south at that time.

"A few of us decided to rent a house in the Hollywood Hills. It worked out great. It had a big yard. We grew our own marijuana. The stuff comes up easy as weeds. We used it just for ourselves between fixes of henry. I couldn't take care of my habit for scag even with my pushing and burning all the time. It cost me over a hundred dollars a day just for my fixes. I couldn't always scratch that kind of juice. Coming down was agony. Going cold turkey is suffering the fires of hell. I got tired of being collared by the fuzz and spending so much time in joints when I was busted for possession of the stuff. The last time I was busted, I was sent to the Mendicino State Hospital in California for treatment. I knew I had to kick the habit for sure or I'd soon be dead. It wasn't easy but I made it. I decided that the important thing in my life now, and this has helped me stay clean, is to help others find themselves. Now my life has meaning and direction. I know that through my own experiences I am helping others. I am doing something constructive instead of self-destructive."

The drug prone

Drug abusers are often intelligent, sensitive, concerned human beings who feel helpless in the world around them. They are unable to cope with the happenings of the present and turn to drugs to stifle their own misgivings and doubts. Distrust, rebellion, hopelessness, and lack of communication cause many to turn inward in drug-induced lethargies of despair in lieu of more constructive action. When these victims of despondency become aware that people do care about them and what happens to them—be it family, friends, peer group, or society in general—the resolve and will to free themselves from drug enslavement is imbued with sincere motivation. At last they find the necessary drive to succeed.

Addiction begins in various ways. Age and ethnic or educational and financial standing do not matter. Hard-drug users are tragically enslaved and think only of their next hits. The unfortunate death recently of a former high-school football star, the son of an outstanding Iowa banker, who destroyed himself while under the mind-shattering influence of a bad LSD trip, caused as much misery and grief to his parents as did the equally tragic death of a thirteen-year-old junkie found lifeless by her mother in their tiny apartment in one of New York City's black ghettos.

Why does today's youth rebel? Why did two youngsters from backgrounds so different and apart both experiment with dangerous drugs?

The underground

One would not expect heroin addicts to emerge from fashionable girls' finishing schools, yet hard-drug users appear in this posh environment all too frequently. Recently two attractive teen-age school friends came to my office. Word had reached them through the drug users' underground grapevine that I treated patients who sincerely desired to get clean. The girls had been roommates at a church boarding school in a Gulf Coast state. Mary and Alice started smoking pot as a lark one weekend when they were bored.

Mary's father is a widely respected senior clergyman and educator in the Protestant faith. Alice's father is a colonel in the United States Armed Forces. Needless to say, the families of both young addicts still don't know that their once-lovely daughters are hooked on heroin, for when the thrill diminished from smoking marijuana these teen-agers experimented with something stronger.

Mary explained as she sat in my office clasping and unclasping her needle-marked hands: "Doctor, I never thought that I would become a junkie. My father and mother are devoted family and church people. I am an only child and have had all the so-called advantages. I was sent to the best schools. As a matter of fact, the headmaster of the boarding school that I attended when I got hooked is a very good friend of my father's. It was at this school that I first saw drugs being used and sold. It was so easy to obtain them. Almost everyone was smoking reefers.

"I felt odd, not part of the scene, not using the marijuana cigarettes as the other kids did. I wanted to be

80

accepted, not referred to as a square. I wanted to make the scene and be liked by the others. It's difficult being a minister's daughter—you have to constantly prove that you are as human as the other kids. I started smoking mary jane [marijuana] when I was fifteen, a couple of years ago. I found it great! It made me feel high. I decided I had to share this goody with Alice. She was and still is my roommate and friend. We started using it the same Saturday afternoon."

Alice, sitting listlessly beside her classmate, nodded. Her voice was low and emotionless as she offered, "We didn't think that rainy Saturday afternoon when we lit our first reefers in our room at school that we'd find ourselves here in your office, more than two thousand miles from home, asking for your help to kick this habit that is destroying us both!"

"We started with a reefer to get high and now must mainline five times a day," resumed Mary, staring at her badly needle-scarred arms and the collapsed veins in her pasty-white, old-woman's hands. "Almost all of us at school were on the stuff just for kicks. Our parents or teachers never warned us about the dangers of drug usage.

"I guess it wouldn't have made much difference. We wanted to be accepted as part of our peer group at school. Getting smack was so easy, we decided that we just had to make the scene."

"We'd mainline scag all over the place," recalled Alice, "and the teachers didn't even seem to know or care. If we needed a fix in a hurry, we'd use a rest room or even a clothes closet off a classroom. Kids would

81

help one another get a shot fast. There never was any trouble getting the stuff at school as long as we had the money to pay for the junk."

"We had good allowances from home," said Mary, "but the habit of mainlining heroin several times a day runs into a real bundle."

Heroin for a single injection may cost anywhere from ten to twenty-five dollars. Prices vary according to the availability of drugs and their quality. If a strict enforcement campaign against smuggling is in process, the supply becomes scarce or dries up, as the addicts put it. Thus prices skyrocket and the quality obtainable may be inferior or more lethal as pushers buy whatever is available. Junkies become desperate and will pay tremendous sums for inferior heroin of unknown potency.

Mary continued: "We'd supplement our income to support our habits by doing things that were real crazy. We'd take anything we could get our hands on. It didn't matter if it was a classmate's monthly allowance or an antique from the school's collection of clocks. When we ran out of things to steal, we'd sneak out after curfew and take to the bars. There are always guys around who would pay well to score with girls from the fashionable finishing school. It flattered their egos that they could make time with us. We didn't care about anything. All we wanted was the money paid in advance that would buy us another fix.

"Somehow, some way that we still can't understand, we graduated from school. All this time, for over a year, our parents and teachers didn't seem to notice any change in us. We knew that terrible things were happening to our minds and bodies. We really didn't care about anything, except for that first sharp stab of the hypo and then the sudden rush and thrill of the stuff flowing in our veins. The ecstasy would last for about a minute, and we'd usually get high for several hours. We'd feel during this time as if we were floating on a cloud.

"We didn't know or care about the past or future. All that mattered was the here and now. We were blissfully content, alone with ourselves, in a world of our very own. This euphoric state would be wonderful, but when the potency of smack would wear off, we'd be miserable. Everything before our eyes would appear drab and gray. We'd start to get nervous spasms in our hands. Our lips were dry and would twitch. We'd feel hot-and-cold tremors all over our bodies. Our legs would tremble, and all our muscles would go into spasms. We would only think how soon we could get another fix and mainline some more stuff into our heroin-starved bodies!

"We really tried to kick the habit. We decided to enroll in the university here, clear across the country from the school we graduated from. We honestly thought that with a new environment we'd get clean!"

"It didn't work out that way," admitted Alice. "We managed to get through the first semester, but halfway through the spring term we became hooked again. Smack is just too easy to get. It's everywhere on the scene. We dropped out of college.

"We are now street people. We both know that if we don't get off the stuff for real, we'll both be dead before our eighteenth birthdays next spring. We can't get enough money to support our heroin needs. We each need over one hundred dollars a day for the junk. We know we have lost our attractiveness. Guys just won't go for us any more. We look like scrawny hags with our pasty-white, acne-blotched complexions and dull, listless eyes. We can't burn enough to keep us in fixes. We are tired of being busted and going cold turkey in jail. We either kick the habit for real or permanently leave this crazy, mixed-up scene!"

Mary nervously touched her dry, colorless lips with her tongue. Alice sighed and concluded, "We've come to you, Doctor, for help. You are our lifeline back to the real world.

"Why me?" I asked.

"Friends have passed the word around that you really care and help us kids medically to kick the habit."

Mary quickly added: "I'll level with you, Doctor. We heard that you are a right guy. You are tough but fair. You don't preach a sermon but expect us to stay off the junk and follow the medical rules. We know that we must stay clean. If we don't, you'll refuse to continue the withdrawal treatment and that will be the end of the line for us!"

"We haven't any more time to kid ourselves," added Alice, slowly rubbing her nose with a needle-scarred hand. "This is the very end for us. We must stop mainlining right now, or we're dead junkies!"

The alienated

The story of John, the son of a prominent Midwestern law professor, has a similar undertone. "If only my parents would have listened to me when I wanted to talk to them, maybe I wouldn't have started floating

84

on the mind detergents [LSD]. The trouble was my folks were so involved in so many good causes that they just didn't have time to talk to me! Almost everyone at school was turned on to something. I felt completely out of the scene. My parents were just too busy to care what I did. I tripped out on acid just for something to do and to be part of the group!"

Lack of communication between parent and youngster may begin in various ways, sometimes so simply that you fail to realize what is happening until it is too late. Your youngster may be looking forward to going with you to a football game or the theatre. Pressing business or a social engagement can force you to suddenly cancel the planned excursion with some vague explanation. Your youngster can't understand how anything can be more important than this event that he or she has been eagerly waiting to share with you. These are the things that all too often alienate them. A wall of distrust begins to form and with it comes a feeling that you are unreliable. They seek and acquire new acquaintances in their own age group who keep their promises, for good or bad. The youngster's sense of values changes abruptly, and they listen to their new companions, who do exactly as they promise.

Now the youngster's life-style begins to change completely. All too often he will no longer show any interest or participation in activities that were formerly an important part of family life. This may develop in a variety of ways. It may be manifested in a sudden sullen refusal to attend religious services or take part in a planned camping trip. Complete indifference to personal appearance and conventional grooming and dress may signal the youth's determined defiance. Your daughter or son may, for example, discard once-cherished clothes for tattered jeans and sandals or bare feet and cultivate the long-haired look and appear unwashed.

This may be simply an outward manifestation of independence, the individual's attempt to assert his defiance of the so-called Establishment. This by itself, though unacceptable and annoying to us and our sense of convention, is not dangerous. What one must be on guard against is that this change in companions and dress may trigger the introduction of a harmful new life-style and the use of dangerous drugs.

Research has shown that when an individual changes his manner of living, his entire set of values as well as his way of life is altered. It may develop gradually over a lengthy period of time, or it may occur abruptly without any prior indication.

Often, youngsters complain less about lack of security or squalid home surroundings than they do about parents who just haven't the time to be concerned with their activities, interests, or problems, who worry more about their golf or bridge scores.

Even a minor slight on the part of an adult, who is often unaware, can easily hurt the youngster who is extremely sensitive. Many times, these young people regard as a personal insult a word harshly spoken or a lack of attention.

The street people
Peter was a sensitive high-school junior with a slight speech defect. Although brilliant, in class he

86

would purposely fail to answer questions in order to avoid his classmates' laughter when he spoke. One day, a substitute teacher, annoyed by his slow, seemingly hesitant reply, unthinkingly called him a stuttering, stupid student. His classmates broke into amused laughter.

Peter never returned to school after that miserable experience. He became instead a recruit of the street people, the unhappy segment of our young who drop out of school, college, and the normal activities of society to live on the streets of our communities. These individuals drift in the euphoria of this underground for various reasons, ranging from an embarrassing acne skin condition to Peter's desire to escape from his unhappy classroom scene and "do his thing." This expression serves as a catch-all for all forms of erratic behavior and covers all the activities of the street people.

They cling to each other in an almost tribal manner. Their entire life-style is based on their closeness—personal as well as financial—to each other. They share food and lodging, when available, as well as a similar manner of dress. At this writing, the mode is American Indian, which features leather dresses, jackets, and trousers, feathered headress, moccasins, boots, and all the other tribal regalia of the early American frontier. It is clearly understood by all participants in the "tribe" that those who possess more worldly goods—be it food, shelter, or drugs—share them with the needy of the clan.

Youngsters surrounded by these seemingly happy and considerate young people find straight society distasteful; in comparison the Establishment appears cruelly unfeeling and perpetually engaged in a rat race for success and status. What they fail to note is that these apparently blissful scenes of love and communal sharing are just as superficial as the Establishment they are so harshly condemning. They seem unaware that robberies, assaults, and murders are an almost daily happening among these seemingly serene street people. The youngsters who so often criticize their parents for lack of communication are unable to establish it with their own peers and don't really understand each other at all.

The best defense against drugs is the love between parents and youngsters who frankly and considerately discuss the differences that often arise in values, hopes, and life-style.

CHAPTER VIII

DOUBLE JEOPARDY:

The Drug War in Vietnam

● ● ● ●

The soaring statistics . . Black-market heroin . . .
Our Government programs . . . The Army Disease
. . . The case against dishonorable discharge. . .

The roaring statistics

Our efforts to help the youth on drugs and his family
would be sadly remiss without a consideration of the
more than sixty-four hundred service personnel to date
who have been discharged from the United States Navy
as hard-drug addicts and the many others like them
in all our Armed Forces. The situation is daily becoming more critical, and the authorities are growing
ever more alarmed by the continuing upsurge of our
servicemen's use of narcotics.

These statistics may startle the layman, but physicians
know that hard-drug usage in the United States Armed
Forces has been an extremely serious problem ever since
the first medical records were kept during the Civil
War. Our servicemen use drugs for the same reasons as
civilians: Pain, stress and tension, fear, loneliness, or
boredom are the primary causes that turn on the first-
time users among them. Once an individual's hesitation

89

and resistance have been overcome, smoking a reefer or mainlining scag no longer appears so sinister or so out of bounds.

When I was serving a tour of duty as a volunteer physician at a civilian hospital in Da Nang, South Vietnam, in 1968, it was common knowledge and an accepted fact of life that our servicemen were smoking reefers and shooting heroin. Some of our combat troops frequently used marijuana before taking off and while on patrol. The despair and frustration that accompany such a change in an individual's life-style may seem eased temporarily by the use of alcohol or drugs. While the exact figures are unobtainable, it has been conservatively estimated by medical experts that anywhere from 50 percent to 80 percent of our service personnel in Southeast Asia use marijuana or more potent drugs. They are cheap and easy to obtain; in some places, marijuana grows wild and soldiers on patrol need only pick it as they pass.

"It is as common as chewing gum here," *Time* Magazine correspondent James Willwerth recently reported from South Vietnam. "The young officers are smoking it nearly as much as the enlisted men."

United States military authorities stated in the fall of 1970 that drugs had already become a serious problem, and more than eleven thousand members of the United States Armed Forces were under investigation during that year for drug usage. In Saigon, one officer of field grade was court-martialed and sentenced to three years in prison for passing pot around to his men. This officer often entertained members of his squadron with marijuana parties in his quarters.

However, what is even more alarming to the American military authorities in Southeast Asia is the ever-increasing use of heroin. Four cases required disciplinary action in 1966 but by 1970 that figure had skyrocketed to over seventeen hundred cases! During one ninety-day period in 1970, more than eighty service personnel died as the result of confirmed or suspected heroin overdosage. It is believed that one in five Americans stationed in Vietnam has experimented with or is now using heroin. Colonel Thornton E. Ireland, the United States provost marshal in Vietnam, was quoted in *Time* Magazine as stating, "We've got a problem. Don't let anyone kid you!"

Military authorities, attempting to stop the spread of marijuana smoking by destroying supplies through aerial searches for the weed and arresting those selling it, unwittingly made it possible for heroin usage to increase alarmingly. Marijuana has a distinctive sweet and pungent scent that often makes it impossible to conceal, whereas heroin is odorless and extremely simple to hide. Service personnel unable to purchase reefers switched to the more dangerous but readily available scag.

Black-market heroin

It is extremely easy to purchase almost any type of drug in Vietnam. This became painfully apparent to the authorities when a huge supply of pure heroin appeared wherever American servicemen were stationed—from the South Vietnam highlands out to its seacoast. Prices ranged from as little as $1.50 for 150 milligrams to three dollars for a small plastic vial of this white, powdery substance. Heroin of comparable quality elsewhere would cost many times that and usually retail for ten dollars to twenty-five dollars a bag. The reason for this low cost is that smack is grown throughout Southeast Asia. Opium poppies are raised in Laos, Thailand, Southern China (for export since Communist China does not approve of the use of opium for its people), and some areas of South Vietnam. The poppy juice is then transported by Asian entrepreneurs to processing centers in Bangkok and Vientiane.

Drugs are easily purchased along the fifteen-mile length of the Bienhoa Highway that extends from Saigon north to Longbinh. Vietnamese children sell heroin from a stand directly opposite the entrance to the headquarters of the largest United States military installation in Vietnam at Longbinh. The stands, set up along the road, usually have no other merchandise, such as fruit or food, on display; the only source of business is the sale of drugs. Soldiers may use cigarettes or military certificates for the purchase price. The cigarettes are then re-sold on the black market by the Vietnamese for many times the $1.75 PX purchase price. The Americans driving the trucks along the highway are good steady customers. They not only purchase the stuff for their own use but for re-sale at a profit.

Some servicemen mix the heroin with cigarette tobacco and smoke it. Others "snort" it, for it can be inhaled as snuff directly into the user's nostrils or sniffed from inhalers. There are areas throughout Southeast Asia where service personnel can obtain and use narcotics in comfortable surroundings. At some Saigon bars, heroin-laced beer can be ordered. There are so-called "private entertainment places" where the customers can shoot heroin or obtain any other drug of their choice—horse, peyote, speed, acid, or bennies.

To worsen the problem, not all the drugs are pure. Dried grass or tea leaves are sometimes added to the marijuana and sugar to the heroin. Frequently needles used in these "shooting galleries" are unclean, accounting for the deadly hepatitis and virulent form of malaria that are being transmitted to others in Southeastern Asia and, in some cases, to the United States.

Unfortunately, there is no simple solution to this ever-increasing grave problem that confronts us overseas and at home. Military courts may court-martial and sentence drug users to penal institutions, but that will not rectify or eradicate the situation. All too often addicts return from prison, civilian and military, more hooked than ever. Guards are frequently pushers of narcotics, and instead of helping the inmates, worsen their drug addiction.

Our Government programs

The military authorities have adopted a humane and realistic approach to this drug epidemic. They have started, with some success, amnesty and education programs. These projects strive to reach service personnel hooked on narcotics and to encourage them to turn themselves in for withdrawal treatment without fear of going to the guardhouse or brig. G.I. radio and television stations here and overseas beam anti-narcotic slogans and announce when and where "rap sessions" are conducted by medical officers and ex-addict servicemen. These open discussions, frank and in the language of drug users, are held in the recreational areas of the various commands. Former addicts serve as counselors and help to bridge the communication gap that separates the drug world from the world of reality.

The program for withdrawal stress usually begins with methadone treatment in an effort to reclaim rather than punish the soldier addict. After a few days, the drug user is introduced to a regimen specially designed to keep him interested and active. He receives points for making his bed, washing an ambulance, working at clerical chores, and attending counseling and rap sessions. The patient is encouraged to earn points, which enable him to obtain more freedom. Upon the successful completion of drug-withdrawal therapy, he can qualify for training as a counselor, a position of great respect and trust. The soldiers who make it and remain off hard drugs are usually the best proselytizers for withdrawal programs.

The program is geared to individual needs. Some drug users are able to kick their habits in weeks, others require months, and some unfortunately go back to their narcotic addiction.

Medical as well as military authorities realize that there is no magic formula or antidote that will immediately cause this disastrous drug epidemic to disappear. It is a product of the times and only through expert medical therapy, counseling, communication, and education can the dangerous situation be quelled.

The Army Disease

Drug problems seem to become critical during wars. The Army Disease, as it was referred to during and after the Civil War, was estimated to have left four hundred thousand veterans of that conflict addicted to morphine.

This natural alkaloid in opium is appropriately named after Morpheus, the Greek god of dreams, for morphine has analgesic properties and was first derived from opium by Serturner in 1803. It was used widely during the Civil War to alleviate pain. As a consequence, the number of morphine addicts in the United States in 1865 was believed to be 1 percent of a population of forty million. Almost all of them were former soldiers whose physicians had indiscriminately prescribed morphine for the relief of pain.

During the Spanish-American War in 1898, no serious drug problem existed. There were other causes of major concern such as improper sanitation and food spoilage. Undoubtedly the short duration of this conflict had much to do with lessening the need for drugs.

Benzedrine, a central nervous-system stimulant first synthesized by Smith, Kline, and French Laboratories in 1927, came into wide use during World War II. This amphetamine-sulfate derivative was issued to soldiers, sailors, and airmen on both sides. Benzedrine made it possible for the users to overcome fatigue and still remain alert and able to perform difficult and tiring tasks for long periods of time. It was first issued to German fliers during the Spanish Civil War in the nineteen-thirties and later became a standard item in survival kits for sailors and airmen. Prolonged use of this stimulant has been extended into civilian life by former servicemen, students, and long-haul drivers who wish to remain awake for long periods of time.

The use of morphine and heroin during the World War I did not prove to be a serious problem. However, since there were ample supplies available during World War II, some service personnel with easy access to medical stores did become addicted to morphine and carried its use over to civilian life. Occasionally, seriously wounded or ill troops were given morphine to alleviate their pain and so became addicted. Almost everyone is familiar with the story of Barney Ross. The champion boxer became hooked by this drug during treatment in a service hospital for wounds received as a World War II Marine and fought valiantly and successfully to kick the habit.

Reason for hope

Thus, what frequently starts as a temporary measure during a period of crisis is carried over to civilian life and becomes a critical addiction. Even though drug usage in the Armed Forces is not a new problem and unfortunately has existed during and after every conflict, we are now more fortunate. The authorities— civilian as well as military—are more aware, and communication and education are available to help the drug users among our servicemen willingly withdraw from their dependence on narcotics.

The problem is by no means licked, but there is reason for hope in that some of our boys wish to be helped. Bill, a patient in an Army withdrawal ward puts it this way, "Man, I was dead, really dead." He had suffered heart stoppage from a heroin overdose and had barely been saved by resuscitation. "I don't want horse to be my bag. I just escaped going home in one!"

The case against dishonorable discharge

It is the responsibility of the United States military authorities to see that the drug users among our service personnel about to be separated from the service receive immediate treatment for addiction at military treatment centers and Veterans' Administration out-patient departments. I do not believe that a brief hospital stay enables an addict to permanently kick the habit. This usually requires a treatment period of weeks or perhaps months. It serves no worthwhile purpose to separate the addict from the world around him for a short time in a hospital and then suddenly thrust him, unprepared, into a seemingly distrustful and hostile society. It is far better to treat the drug abuser as an out-patient for it makes the necessary transition easier for the patient and the family. It also enhances the chances of successful withdrawal treatment, thus making it far more promising for the patient, the family, and the community.

The servicemen who until recently were given dishonorable discharges for drug addiction should be treated by the V.A. as ill instead of being dishonored and branded as criminals. They, too, should be treated for drug addiction at the veterans' centers, and the stigma of dishonorable discharge should be erased from their records. They are human beings badly in need of help, and it is the responsibility of the Government to help the drug users who want it. The servicemen addicts who received dishonorable discharges prior to the recent Government change of policy are entitled to the same consideration and help as the drug abusers now being separated from the Armed Forces. Only in this

97

manner can the military authorities gain the confidence and trust of the servicemen who are hooked on narcotics and yet understandably hesitate to seek help. Over and over again, I hear from my patients—many of them former G.I.'s who served in Vietnam, although a few brought the drug habit with them when they went into service—the same doubtful words: "How can we trust them [the Government] to help us when they gave the other guys dishonorable discharges? What's to prevent us getting the same rough deal after they know that we are junkies?"

PART II

●　　●　　●　　●

Tell Me, Doctor!

1. Tell me, Doctor, will the heroin habit affect normal sex relations?

   Definitely! Addicts on heroin have no desire or energy to engage in sex relations. The drug user nods while on a fix and the rest of his time is spent in hassling for enough bread to get the next!

2. Is there any hope for a junkie that has been mainlining for years to live a normal family life after he comes off heroin?

   Yes, there is! However, you must remember that much depends upon the individual and his or her determination to make a complete break with the former life-style and become a contributing member of society with regular work and life patterns. Many of my patients have proved to themselves that this is possible. One young man of twenty-two is the proud father of a baby boy and is working fifty hours a week in a copper mine. He is buying a home and is a true believer in the methadone therapy that has helped him make this possible. Two years ago, he was one of the biggest heroin wholesalers in town.

3. If heroin users are not interested in sex, why then are there junkie prostitutes?

Male and female junkie prostitutes roam the city streets for only one reason—heroin. They are intent on selling their bodies in order to obtain bread to buy smack. Sex means nothing to them. They do not enjoy sex; it is the only means available to them for obtaining money for the monkeys on their backs.

4. If a teen-ager starts using heroin, will it affect sexual development?

That depends upon many factors concerning the individual such as age when the habit started— at the onset of puberty, before or after, and the type of habit. I will explain it in this manner. Youngsters of nine or ten using heroin will have less chance of normal sexual development than those who started at sixteen or seventeen. One who is a "chipper," and uses it occasionally will suffer far less than one who uses heroin five or six times a day.

5. How long after an addict begins methadone therapy does the desire for sex return?

There are no set rules. However, usually it is only a matter of a few days before normal sex desires return to the patient.

6. Does the use of heroin have any prolonged or lasting effect on the child of a pregnant addict?

It most certainly does! Here in Tucson, babies born to Yaqui Indian mothers often have to be treated for heroin withdrawal at birth.

7. How can the physician determine if the baby needs withdrawal treatment?

Experience is the best teacher! The Yaqui Indians are known to be heroin users. Unfortunately, it is very often part of their way of life. They obtain the drugs from their relatives through regular established channels in Mexico. They are of Mexican origin and have been in Arizona since 1912 when a change in Government caused them to leave and come across the border. Since most adults in the Yaqui community use heroin, it is reasonable to assume that women coming to the hospital should be examined for the usual signs of addiction such as needle-marks, apathy, stress, and anxiety. When the attending physician determines that the expectant mother is on heroin, immediate action is taken to save the life of the unborn child.

8. What withdrawal therapy is used to treat the infant?

Immediately after birth, the infant is examined by a special team of medical experts skilled in the management of this difficult problem. Usually it is headed by a pediatrician and staffed by several nurses specially trained in infant care. Since most babies born to mothers addicted to heroin are premature as well as hooked on drugs, there are many problems in their care if they are to survive. An infant that is born addicted to heroin usually has watery eyes, a running nose, a nervous twitching of its body, and a shrill, piercing cry that once heard is unforgettable and far different from that of a normal newborn. The baby must immediately be treated with camphorated opium tincture. This process of de-sensitization or withdrawal usually requires two to four weeks. The infant is given one to two drops of camphorated opium in its formula until it gradually withdraws from the addiction it acquired in its mother's womb prior to its birth. The dosage is not to exceed three or four drops a day.

9. Won't the infant again acquire the heroin habit from its mother if it is breast fed?

   No! Fortunately addicts on heroin are unable to breast-feed their babies and can't poison them with drugged milk.

10. Isn't it dangerous for women on heroin to have babies?

    It certainly is not recommended as the best way to start an infant in life. As mentioned before, women addicted to heroin almost always give birth to premature infants.

11. If addicts aren't interested in sex while on heroin, how do they get pregnant?

    Sometimes between hits they feel normal desires for a time and that's how it happens.

12. Do junkies make good parents?

    Yes, they do! They care very deeply for their children and are usually devoted parents.

13. Do the heroin addicts' children know that the parents are drug users?

No, not usually. The parents try to keep the secret of their addiction from their youngsters.

14. Does a woman heroin user have normal periods?

A female heroin user frequently misses periods due to hormone imbalance because of drug usage. Often she will mistakenly believe that she is pregnant.

15. When a woman heroin addict stops using the drug and starts methadone therapy, will her periods then become normal?

It is usually necessary to prescribe female estrogenic substances (hormones) by injection or orally over a period of days. The normal periods usually return three to ten days after the final heroin injection or medication has been given if the patient is not pregnant!

16. Do women heroin addicts lose their looks?

It depends upon their habits. If a user "chips" and does not mainline daily, there is far less chance of her becoming blowsy. However, if she scores several hits a day, she becomes listless, careless in personal appearance, and suffers from malnutrition with the resulting sallow or acne-marked complexion.

17.   Is it true that women addicts sometimes use their body orifices to smuggle heroin across the border?

Yes, women heroin users sometimes attempt to smuggle an ounce or two of pure heroin wrapped in double plastic bags hidden in their vaginas. They receive a fourth of the amount as payment if they manage to smuggle it across the border. However, quite often they fail in their attempt, for the United States has specially trained female customs inspectors who are expert in handling situations such as these. I recall one former smack user who complained bitterly about her thorough examination at the Nogales inspection station. She was made to stand on her head while a lady inspector and registered nurse probed for secret stashes of heroin.

18.   Do men attempt to smuggle drugs across the border hidden on them?

Yes, when the heat is on and heroin is difficult to come by, some pushers in desperation will attempt to smuggle a couple of ounces across the border by filling balloons with smack and swallowing it. This is extremely dangerous, for if the rubber balloon bursts before it is removed from the stomach of the carrier, death will come very quickly from overdosage of this huge amount of uncut heroin.

19. How does the courier remove the heroin-filled balloon from his stomach?

It must be removed within four to six hours or the gastric juices in the courier's stomach will start to dissolve the rubber encasing the heroin. An emetic—usually a solution of mustard and water or salt and water—is used by the drug courier to regurgitate the rubber balloon. This is a dangerous procedure, for if it becomes lodged in the individual's throat, he or she may strangle to death before it can be removed.

20. Is this a very successful means of smuggling heroin into United States?

No! This is used only when other sources "dry up." Heroin smugglers do not wish to use themselves in this manner if other means of transporting the stuff are available.

21. Is it difficult to detect drug smugglers crossing the border?

It is extremely difficult. There is no such thing as the look of a drug smuggler. Quite often, the so-called hippie types will deliberately, while on drug-courier missions, pretend to be straight. They will wear conservative clothes, submit to haircuts, and seem to be just the same as other tourists crossing the border.

22. Does this drug problem occur elsewhere in the world?

Yes! Unfortunately it seems to be universal and is not unique to the United States. President Georges Pompidou of France appealed to the other countries in the Common Market and to Britain for cooperation in fighting the drug plague, which he emphasized first appeared in the United States and is now on the increase in all of Europe.

23. Is this problem as serious overseas as in the United States?

It is extremely serious throughout the world. A British educator recently told of seeing young hippies from the United States and Europe wander around cities and towns in Afghanistan "begging like dogs" for hashish and selling their bodies for a fix. They have become dependent on scraps of food, contemptuous objects of charity, begging for a daily supply of hashish or other narcotics provided by Afghans who treat them as weird human pets. The hippies, who set out with dreams and fantasies of reaching an illusory promised land, have become broken and as smashed as so many worthless garbage cans. Such is the effect of hashish. These addicts sell all their possessions, their bodies, and their girl friends to buy drugs.

24. What can be done to stop this drug plague?

Education and legislation will stop the use of harmful drugs throughout the world.

25. Tell me, Doctor, is the use of alcohol considered addictive?

It depends upon the individual. It is considered addictive if the user cannot function without the use of alcohol and it becomes a crutch upon which the patient depends.

26. Is alcoholism a recent product of the times?

No! Many people are unaware that alcoholics have been a problem to themselves and society almost since the beginning of recorded history. Alcohol is a narcotic drug that we sometimes forget is addictive.

27. What is being done to overcome alcoholism in this country?

President Nixon has requested that Congress appropriate $50 million (at the same time that $250 million is budgeted to treat heroin addiction with methadone) to combat alcoholism in the United States.

28. Is it true that some areas have a much higher average of alcoholics than others?

Yes, for some unknown reason that happens to be true. It is estimated by experts in this field that out of the slightly more than 700,000 population of San Francisco approximately 150,000 residents are confirmed or borderline alcoholics.

29. Is the current widespread drug abuse a new problem in this country?

No! Many of us are unaware that during Prohibition in the nineteen-twenties and early thirties there was an extremely serious national problem with the flappers of that era. They were addicted to drinking alcohol or "booze" because it was against the law, in much the same manner as today's youth abuses drugs. There were many deaths among those in the flapper age group, as well as among their elders, from the use of wood alcohol in the booze. This era also gave rise to gang wars, the highjacking of booze deliveries, and the appearance of the underworld or organized crime in our society. Addiction to alcohol is just as much a problem as the misuse of drugs.

30. What is the difference between addiction to drugs and addiction to alcohol?

They are equally dangerous if misused. If properly used under competent professional guidance, they often serve a beneficial purpose as stimulants or tranquilizers. However, alcohol is readily available at liquor stores, and since both Federal and state governments derive revenue tax from its sale, almost everyone of legal age can obtain it. Thus, although it is just as addictive if used in large quantities, many of today's youth prefer drugs simply because they are more difficult to obtain. This makes it more thrilling and exciting to use or abuse.

31. Is it true that American Indians have drug and alcohol problems?

Yes, unfortunately this is quite true. The American Indians sometimes use peyote, mescaline, and morning-glory seeds as well as other derivatives of cactus plants in their religious celebrations. Often these drugs produce psychotic reactions similar to those caused by the use of LSD. Alcoholism is a very serious problem among the Indians of the American Southwest. Several years ago a young Indian World War II hero, a winner of the Congressional Medal of Honor, died of acute alcoholism on his home reservation in Arizona.

32. Does prolonged use of alcohol cause an increase in the suicide rate?

Definitely! The suicide rate among Indian youth is twice as high as the national average. The same facts appear in San Francisco among all age groups because a serious drinking problem exists there.

33. Have these drinking and drug problems been unique to the United States?

No! Eighteenth-century London had a critical gin epidemic. The poor in London around 1750 were drinking eleven million gallons of gin annually, simply to escape from the anxiety and tension of their times. They lived in squalor and took to alcohol abuse to escape from the filth and overcrowding in their slum environment. Country people had crowded into London and discovered that life was difficult and work hard to come by. Gin was cheap and as a result they drugged themselves with alcohol to forget

113

for a time their many problems. Nutrition of the poor was extremely bad and the mortality rate of infants born to the gin addicts was extremely high. More than 50 percent of all newborn babies died. Now, problems of drug addiction and acute alcoholism exist all over the world.

34. What are other countries doing about the drug plague?

Fortunately, now, as the authorities see that this is a worldwide epidemic, they are taking action to prevent the smuggling, distribution, and use of drugs within their borders and shipment of these harmful items to other countries. President Georges Pompidou of France requested international governmental conferences twice a year to trade and coordinate information to combat this epidemic.

35. Are the drug laws in other countries enforced as tightly as they are in the United States?

The drug laws in Europe, Mexico, and in the Far East are a great deal tougher than ours. In Mexico, possession of illegal drugs can result in a prison sentence of from two to nine years. Carrying illicit drugs will automatically result in a jail sentence of from six to fifteen years. Drug arrests of young Americans around the world have increased 70 percent since 1970. At this time over seven hundred United States citizens are serving time on charges of illegal possession of drugs in prisons in other countries.

36. If a former heroin user switches to methadone therapy when she discovers that she is pregnant, will her unborn child need to be treated for withdrawal at birth?

Usually, if a former heroin addict gives up her habit and undergoes methadone therapy prior to three months of term, the infant will not have to be treated for withdrawal. The baby may be slightly premature, usually a week or two, but will not be addicted to heroin.

37. Will the baby need methadone therapy at birth?

No! Except in some slightly premature cases, the infant should be normal and not suffer from any adverse conditions.

38. Is alcohol ever used medicinally?

Yes, quite often a glass of sherry or some other wine or liquor may be prescribed by a physician for its tranquilizing or mildly stimulating effect. It is not the use but the abuse of drugs and alcohol that is producing worldwide problems. Today, in many areas of this country, the medication of choice by pediatricians to calm restless babies is to include in the infants' formulas one or two drops of whiskey.

39. Are drugs ever safe to use?

Drugs properly prescribed and administered are extremely effective and necessary in the treatment of illness. It is the misuse and abuse of these products that is extremely dangerous.

40. Doctor, is it wise to suddenly deprive patients undergoing methadone therapy of their medication? Sometimes a former drug abuser is arrested and held in jail for a hearing and the methadone tablets in the patient's possession are confiscated. Do you approve of these methods?

I most certainly do not! This is cruel and inhuman punishment. Patients should not be made to suffer the agonies of withdrawal and denied methadone or tranquilizers that are prescribed by their physicians. If a drug abuser is being held in jail and suffering from the pangs of withdrawal, the physician of the prison should be authorized by the authorities to prescribe methadone, tranquilizers, or other necessary medication to ease the acute agony of withdrawal. We are not living in the Dark Ages and should have compassion and understanding for others' problems. These sick individuals should not be treated as criminals but should be educated and helped instead.

41. Why are amphetamines subject to Federal Government regulations?

These synthetic amines produce a stimulating effect on the central nervous system if properly prescribed and used. Unfortunately, however, the abuse of this group of stimulants has resulted in an increasing number of fatalities due to misuse. On August 5, 1971, new regulations placed the issuance of all prescriptions of this group under the Federal Narcotic Control Act. A new prescription signed by the physician with his narcotic-license number, together with the patient's name, must be on every prescription order. Automatic refills are no longer permitted. These stringent new regulations have been enacted to guard against the ever-increasing use of these "uppers," or speed, by youngsters and thrill seekers who often experiment their way into the morgue.

42. When are amphetamines used for beneficial results?

As I mentioned earlier, amphetamines, when used properly under competent medical supervision, produce excellent results in weight control and enable the dieter to suppress his or her appetite. It is believed that this medication provides a feeling of well-being and depresses appetite by action of the hypothalamus. Amphetamines are also sometimes the drug of choice in the treatment of manic-depressive or schizoid psychoses as well as narcolepsy and related central nervous-system illnesses. The amount prescribed for treatment varies from fifteen to thirty milligrams daily. Occasionally, as in the treatment of narcolepsy, the dosage may be increased over a period of time to fifty milligrams. However, it must be remembered that this extremely high dosage without tolerance being increased over a period of time can often trigger a severe psychosis in the drug abuser with paranoid delusions and hallucinations.

43.   Does the misuse of amphetamines cause drug abusers to commit and become involved in accidents and crimes of violence?

Yes, amphetamines are often the cause of crimes of shocking violence and carnage in highway accidents. The grisly Sharon Tate murders in Beverly Hills by the so-called Manson Tribe have been said to have been committed while the cult members were under the influence of speed, LSD, and some cactus derivatives. These are all mind-shattering if used in excessive amounts. Together they produce toxic psychosis with hallucinations and paranoid delusions that turn the users into human monsters. Dependence upon amphetamines to combat tiredness may cause not only a serious habit but severe depression that may result in suicide. The long-haul truckdrivers who are independent contractors and work on a tight time schedule often stay awake for twenty hours or more by popping uppers or speed, and are far more often involved in fatal accidents than drivers who do not resort to these pep pills. The extra bursts of energy they give exact their toll from the user not only in dependence but in ill health. The side effects that these drugs produce through overdosage include severe fatigue when the effects finally wear off, acute depression, serious gastrointestinal disturbance, general weakness, nervous tremors, dilated eye pupils, dry nose and mouth, and frequent aggressive paranoid behavior.

44. Tell me, Doctor, is it true that amphetamines are sometimes used by authors, composers, and even pilots to stimulate alertness and wakefulness?

Yes, this is quite true. It is a well-known fact that during World War II ferry pilots flying bombers from this country to Britain had in their survival kits one of the amphetamine group —most often Benzedrine, or bennies. Occasionally one of the others such as Dexedrine, Methedrine, Desbutal, Desoxyn, or Dexamyl would be used. The usage of these pep pills was not restricted to fliers. They were used by the commandos on both sides, as well as by ground troops, when great physical endurance for forced marches and other superhuman efforts were required.

Amphetamines are sometimes used by authors, composers, actors, engineers, students—almost anyone who is engaged for a prolonged period of time in exacting mental work. These drugs are resorted to, and most often abused, to stimulate alertness and keenness of the mental processes. However, while prolonged wakefulness occurs, this does not prevent errors in judgment. Amphetamines stimulate wakefulness and the mental process but do not increase accurate performance. Prolonged usage will result in drug dependence followed by exhaustion, aggressiveness, and possibly even paranoia. One cannot continue indefinitely to force one's self to the brink of physical and mental endurance and not expect to pay the price of a complete breakdown.

45. Why are amphetamines said to appeal to a wide range of users, from those seeking sex kicks to speed freaks?

Amphetamines vary in side effects and potency and each has its cult of users. Methedrine is extremely popular with confirmed users who frequently inject it intravenously. This produces almost immediately a "rush" that many users compare to an orgasm, yet this drug sometimes reacts differently and delays sexual orgasm. The heroin abuser occasionally uses amphetamines together with heroin for a special rush. Users of this often are extremely excited, have feelings of great power, and frequently engage in violent and often destructive acts. They suffer from insomnia and are often paranoid enough to commit murder, as occurred in several recent cases in California. They are frequently called by other addicts speed or meth freaks because of their bizarre conduct and actions.

Methedrine, known chemically as methamphetamine hydrochloride or d-desoxyephedrine hydrochloride, is manufactured in this country by Burroughs Wellcome, and Company. It was first used by the Germans in World War II to overcome extreme fatigue in troops that had to forgo sleep for long periods of time. It is considered a more powerful stimulant than Benzedrine and Dexedrine. Under proper medical supervision, Methedrine is used in dieting as an appetite depressant, to raise extremely low blood pressure, and as an analeptic (stimulant) in cases of overdosage of barbiturates and chronic depression. Methedrine is subject to the Narcotic Act of August 5, 1971. It is sold by prescription only in twenty-milligram ampsules for injection and as five-milligram tablets. Addicts refer to an injection of heroin and cocaine or amphetamine as a "speedball."

Dexamyl, another member of the amphetamine group, is composed of d-amphetamine sulfate and amobarbital. It is both a central nervous-system stimulant and depressant. It has euphoric qualities and acts as an appetite depressant. The barbiturate combined with the amphetamine serves to balance any overstimulation caused by the amphetamine. Medically it is prescribed as a mood elevator and appetite depressant in dieting. It is manufactured by Smith, Kline, and French Laboratories, and is prescribed in time-release spansules, tablets, and as a liquid. Overdosage or prolonged use may cause addiction. This may result in severe depression or stimulation to the user.

Dexedrine, another stimulant of the amphetamine group, is twice as powerful as any of the others. Its chemical composition is d-amphetamine sulfate. This potent mood elevator is used for the treatment of depression as well as narcolepsy and alcoholism, and also serves as a depressant for those anxious to lose weight. This, too, is a product of Smith, Kline, and French Laboratories. It stimulates the central nervous system, and dependence may develop after prolonged or unnecessary use.

Desbutal, methamphetamine hydrochloride and pentobarbital sodium, is manufactured by Abbot Laboratories. This is a barbiturate combined with an amphetamine for use in dieting and as a mood elevator. The amphetamine depresses the appetite and stimulates the central nervous system. The barbiturate elevates the mood of the user and serves as a sedative. Prolonged usage may cause dependence. This diet drug is exceedingly popular in Hollywood where weight control is always a problem. Recently actress Jane Fonda was arrested with several thousand amphetamines of various types in her possession. She readily admitted that she used them constantly to keep her weight under control. Of course, these, like all the amphetamines, are strictly controlled under the new Federal narcotic regulations of August 5, 1971, as dangerous and habit-forming drugs.

Desoxyn, methamphetamine hydrochloride, is another product of Abbot Laboratories. This drug of the amphetamine group works as a stimulant on the central nervous system of the user. It is used in dieting to depress the appetite and for mood elevation in the treatment of alcoholism, depression, and narcolepsy. Prolonged usage may cause dependence and such psychotic problems as extreme depression or violent agitation. Desoxyn, too, comes under the Dangerous Drug Act and Regulations of August 5, 1971.

46. What is the difference between methadone and Dolophine?

There is no difference, and the names are interchangeable. Dolophine is the trade name for methadone hydrochloride, a product of Eli Lilly and Company. In Great Britain, where methadone is often used in drug-withdrawal treatment centers, it is frequently called physeptone.

47. Does methadone cause the same euphoria or dulling of the senses as heroin?

No, fortunately it does not cause the user to "drop out." When used as an analgesic, it is often more potent than morphine with effects lasting from three to four hours, but it does not produce a sedative effect, nodding, or a state of euphoria as would morphine. I have patients on methadone therapy (for heroin-addiction withdrawal) who must be constantly alert in their work. Among them are a C.P.A., a teaching fellow in English, a driver of a 150-ton ore truck, and a machinist who works with tools that measure tensions to 3/10,000 of an inch. It is quite apparent that methadone does not dull the user's reasoning powers.

48. Why do some young people—Dr. James Pike's son and Arthur Linkletter's daughter, for example—become victims of drug abuse?

It is indeed unfortunate that so many of today's youth become addicted to drugs before the danger signs are recognized. Dr. Pike's son was treated for mental depression with LSD in the early nineteen-sixties by a psychiatrist in San Francisco. It was believed at that time by the staff psychiatrists at the University of California School of Medicine that LSD was helpful in the treatment of mental depression. However, as in young Mr. Pike's case, the reverse proved true. He became hooked to this hallucinogenic drug, sank ever deeper into a depressive state, and took his own life.

Arthur Linkletter's daughter is reported to have dived out of a sixth-story window. It appears that she was under the influence of a hallucinogenic drug, probably LSD. Often users of lysergic acid suffer from a complete disassociation with reality. They think that they can fly and, without fear, attempt to jump from heights and float through the air. They suffer from distortions of time and space and are often powerless to resist impulses that are self-destructive; hence the expression a "bad trip."

49. Tell me, Doctor, are some of these tough-type motorcyclists addicted to drugs?

Yes, there are some special clubs where members engage in various activities peculiar to their groups. This often includes homosexuality accompanied by the use of speed with beer or whiskey chasers.

50. How can these motorcyclists keep their sense of balance when they are on drugs?

They can't. Quite often they are involved in serious or fatal accidents because of errors of judgment due to the use of drugs and alcohol, a dangerous combination. The accident rate is much higher than average due to the use of these mind-altering drugs.

51. Does the use of drugs cause these motorcyle club members to become violent and behave aggressively?

Yes, the use of speed often causes unpredictable bizarre behavior in users. They frequently become violent and fight with tire irons, clubs, chains, and tear up places as well as themselves; hence the name "speed or meth freaks." These bloody encounters often end in murder.

52. Doctor, is it true that some people can get high from smoking dried bananas, nutmeg, cinnamon, and green peppers?

It may be possible if not probable. Some users of these exotic substances believe that they have mind-altering properties, and since they believe that these substances will affect their consciousness, they may. Quite often the desired effect is created in the mind of the user, and the smoking of a corn-silk cigarette will produce the same high for the believer as a reefer if he or she so wills it.

53. Which is more addictive and dangerous to use, hashish or marijuana?

Hashish and marijuana are both derived from cannabis sativa—the hemp plant. Hashish is much more addictive and dangerous. I am not an advocate of the use of marijuana, for many of my patients have told me that after using reefers they decided to try heroin. Marijuana, however, is not as enslaving nor does it produce the many dangerous side effects of hashish. Marijuana is about only a tenth as potent as hashish, and marijuana grown in America is mild compared to that grown in the Middle and Far East, North Africa, and India. Marijuana may produce a mild hallucinogenic state in the user; hashish, on the other hand, may cause violent distortions, maddening hallucinations, and paranoia.

54. Tell me, Doctor, are drugs such as tranquilizers responsible for ill effects? Can some users become dependent on them?

Tranquilizers or any other medication when used properly under professional direction and supervision are extremely helpful in treating illness. It is only when the use is abused by the individual who decides that he or she will take a certain drug without professional authorization that difficulties often arise. The point here is that drugs are often blamed for a result that an individual has brought about through abuse. All too often, a well-meaning individual will urge his or her friend to try medication that was not intended for the use of anyone but the patient. Too many pills are handed out as candy by some individuals to their friends. It can sometimes be fatal if an individual who has had methedrine prescribed as an appetite depressant to lose weight urges someone with cardiac disease or high blood pressure to pop speed for a thrill.

55. Do you think that children should be given tranquilizers to calm them down as the authorities do in some schools in California?

Absolutely no! Youngsters should not be given tranquilizers except in some conditions such as hyperexcitability, and then only after the parents and family physicians are consulted and agree. I do not believe youngsters should be overmedicated.

56.   What type of tranquilizers are given to young-
       sters in school?

       Ritalin in five-mg. tablets once or twice a day
       are sometimes prescribed by the school doctor
       and given by the school nurse or teacher to
       youngsters who appear to be "too active," with-
       out the consent or knowledge of their parents.
       These tranquilizers should never be given to
       children without the permission of their parents
       and family doctors. Unnecessary or overmedica-
       tion is often the first step on the downward path
       to drug addiction. There is definitely a difference
       in the proper usage of drugs in the treatment of
       illness and the prescribing of tranquilizers as so
       much candy in the calming of active youngsters.
       Children must play, and only the parents and
       family physicians can decide when and if medi-
       cation is indicated for hyperexcitability.

57.   Doctor, I have heard that since the ampheta-
       mines have been misused, even by those on
       weight-reduction programs, stringent laws have
       been enacted to make it extremely difficult to
       obtain any amphetamines. What is being pre-
       cribed instead?

       New Federal regulations on August 5, 1971,
       placed the amphetamines in the same dangerous
       drug category as narcotics, and rightly so. Rita-
       lin in ten-mg. tablets three times daily are being

prescribed instead of amphetamines for weight reduction.

58. Didn't you mention that Ritalin is given as a tranquilizer?

Yes, this is quite true. Medications properly administered frequently serve more than one purpose. Ritalin is used both as an appetite depressant in dieting and as a tranquilizer.

59. Is it true that prolonged dependence on amphetamines can cause a person to drop dead or behave as a maniac and have paranoid delusions?

Unfortunately, this is true. Quite often one hears about an athlete who seemingly has just "dropped dead" from overexertion. Usually the victim has been a long-time user or abuser of some form of pep pills that he or she has taken to create a feeling of strength and well-being, to overcome fatigue, and increase performance and endurance. The user is forcing his or her body beyond the working point of its physical limits. Heart action and blood pressure are greatly increased, and death may result from a complete physical breakdown or suicide.

Amphetamine users recently have been associated with gruesome crimes of extreme violence. The murderer of several student nurses in Chicago a few years ago, a man named Speck, confessed to the police that he had been on speed and used alcohol as a chaser. He went berserk, attacked the young nurses with knives, and turned the students' quarters into a bloody slaughterhouse. Speck added that he did not even remember how he started on his path of madness that day that transformed the nurses' residence into a gruesome and gory place of death.

On the August night that the exclusive and secluded mansion of actress Sharon Tate in the hills above Beverly Hills, California, was invaded by the drugged followers of Charles (Charlie) Manson, five people, including Miss Tate, were brutally murdered. During the next few days, more innocent people were slaughtered by these speed freaks. The final count of murders by this group may never be known, for as Charles (Tex) Watson, one of the defendants on trial in Los Angeles, confessed in open court, he and the others were under the influence of the hallucinatory drugs, belladonna, LSD, and speed. Watson was unable to think for himself and carried out the murder instructions of Charlie Manson, guru and self-styled Jesus, to "kill everybody there as gruesomely as you can." They continued on their murder sprees in Southern California for months, returning to their headquarters at a ranch in the desert to get high on drugs and plan their next expeditions of death.

According to Watson's confession, he was "in a kind of mass form, like I was half-awake." He said during his recital of the events leading to the gruesome Sharon Tate killings, "I could hear Charlie and his voice telling me to kill everybody."

There never can be an excuse for murder or any crime, and the explanation that the drug abusers were high on LSD, speed, or any other hallucinatory agents is not a defense for violence in my opinion. The best means of avoiding harm to themselves as well as to others is not to use any manner of drugs without expert medical advice. Drugs prescribed by physicians are to be used *by the patient* and *only as directed.*

We know that both LSD and speed can produce a wildly hallucinatory condition with acute paranoia and an extreme aggressiveness that approaches madness. Belladonna is used by some cults that indulge in witchcraft for the bizarre effects produced by the atropine in the roots and leaves of this deadly plant of the nightshade group. The members of the Manson cult used all of these before venturing forth on their gory forays.

GLOSSARY OF SLANG TERMS ASSOCIATED WITH TODAY'S YOUTH AND THE DRUGS THEY ABUSE

ACAPULCO GOLD
A form of marijuana. Grown near Acapulco, Mexico.

ACID
LSD, Lysergic acid diethylamide.

ACID HEAD
LSD user. Same as acid freak.

AMPING, OVER-AMPING
O.D. Overdose of drugs.

WHERE IT'S AT
Where drug action is taking place. Sale and/or/use.

BABYSIT
To guide a person through his drug experience by a confirmed user.

BACKWARDS
Tranquilizers. Used to calm LSD and speed addicts.

BAG
Container of drugs. Usually heroin or life style.

FINDING YOUR BAG
See Doing your thing. An addict's way of life.

BALLOON
Rubber toy balloon used for storing or delivering narcotics, usually capped heroin in bulk form but occasionally papered or capped.

BARBS
Barbiturates. May be hypnotic or sedative.

BENNIES, BEANS
Amphetamines. Benzedrine tablets.

BINDLE
A small paper packet of heroin, morphine, cocaine, or methedrine.

BLAST, BLOW
To smoke a marijuana cigarette.

BLOW YOUR MIND
To get high or on drugs.

BLUE BANDS	Pentobarbital Sodium.
BLUE CHEER	Type of LSD.
BLUE BIRDS,	Amobarbital capsules (amytal;
BLUE DEVILS,	amorbarbital sodium). This also
BLUE HEAVEN,	describes pale-blue color of drugs.
BLUES	
BOGART	(From Humphrey Bogart.) To "Bogart a joint" is either to salivate on or to retain (and not pass around) a marijuana cigarette.
BOMBED	Intoxicated on drugs. Freaked out.
BOO	Cannabis. Marijuana.
BOOSTER	Consumption or injection of additional dosage to continue or prolong a trip on drugs.
BOTTLE DEALER	A person who sells drugs in 1000-tablet or capsule bottles.
BREAD	Money.
BRICK	Kilo of marijuana in compressed brick form.
BRIDGE	*See* Crutch. Usually alligator clamp or like device used to hold marijuana cigarette while smoking same.
BUMMER, BUM TRIP	A bad trip. *See* Freak trip, Freak out. Bad drug experience.
BURN	To accept money and give no drug in return, or to give a substance in lieu of the drug; also, to burn the skin when injecting. Stealing to pay for drug habit.
BURNED	Used to describe the acquisition of bad drugs, diluted drugs, or no drugs at all or stealing to buy drugs.
BUTTON	Peyote buttons containing the psychedelic, mescaline.

BUY	To purchase drugs.
CAN	One ounce of marijuana. Term derived from tobacco can in which marijuana was commonly sold in the past. Now, it is more frequently sold in small plastic or paper bags. May also refer to heroin or morphine.
CANDY	Barbiturates. Cocaine or heroin.
CAP	Capsule containing drugs. May be heroin, morphine or LSD.
CARGO	Load of supply of narcotics or drugs.
CARRYING	In possession of drugs. Usually narcotics.
CARTWHEEL	Amphetamine tablet (round, white, double scored).
CENTS	C.C.'s, Cubic centimeter or one dollar.
CHALK	Methamphetamine. White amphetamine tablet.
CHICKEN POWDER	Amphetamine powder for injection.
CHIP, CHIPPY CHIPPER	Using drugs sporadically. Not a daily user.
CHRISTMAS TREE	Tuinal. Contains equal amounts of Amytal (blue and orange) and seconal.
CLEAN	To remove stems and seeds from marijuana; also refers to an addict who is free from needle-injection marks; also, not holding or possessing any narcotics.
COCKTAIL	A regular cigarette into one end of which a partially smoked marijuana cigarette is inserted so as to waste none of the drug.

COKE	Cocaine.
COLD TURKEY	Trying to break the habit. "Kicking it cold turkey" is breaking the habit of addictive drug use at home, in prison, etc., without the aid of any medication or medical care or assistance.
COME DOWN	To come off of drugs.
CONNECT	To buy drugs.
CONNECTION	Refers to the peddler or source of supply for the user.
CONTACT HIGH	A feeling of being on drugs or "high" from merely being in contact with someone or something reminding one of drugs.
COOKER	Bottle cap for heating drug powder with water. Usually heroin.
COOL	Groovy. High on drugs.
COP, TO COP	To get drugs or to admit guilt.
COPE	To handle oneself effectively while under the influence of drugs.
CO-PILOTS	Amphetamines. Also someone who guides an LSD user on a trip.
CRASH	To end a drug experience, particularly from an amphetamine like methedrine. To sleep off drugs.
CRASH PAD	Temporary residence, usually for a night or two, usually communal, often used to end a drug experience or share one.
CRAZY	Exciting, in the know, enjoyable.
CRUTCH	Device used to hold marijuana cigarette when it has burned to the point where it will burn the fingers—usually a half of a paper

	matchbook; also a container for a hypodermic needle.
CRYSTAL	Methedrine (methamphetamine), speed, or other amphetamine.
CRYSTALS	Amphetamine powder for injection.
CUBE	Sugar cube impregnated with LSD.
CUT	To dilute a powder with milk, sugar, baking powder, etc. as heroin.
"D"	LSD.
DEALER	A drug peddler. Pusher.
DEUCE BAG	A two-dollar container of a drug.
DEXIES	Dextroamphetamine sulfate amphetamine tablets, a mixture of barbiturate and amphetamine. Dexedrine capsules.
DMT	Dimethyltryptamine, a psychedelic rapidly acting hallucinogenic similar to the "magic mushrooms." Occasionally marijuana.
DIME or DIME BAG	Ten dollar's worth of heroin.
DOING	May be any happening, but specifically the taking of a drug.
DOING YOUR THING	Doing what seems best to you; finding your bag or thing.
DOPE	Any drug.
DOPER	Drug user.
DOTTING	Placing LSD on a sugar cube.
DOUBLE CROSS	Amphetamine tablets (double scored).
DOWNER	Depressant drugs such as barbiturates or tranquilizers; also, a "bum trip"; to come off drugs.
DREAMER	One who takes opiates or morphine. Any drug user.

FAT	Describing someone who has a good supply of drugs.
FINE STUFF	Drugs of unusually good quality, or only slightly adulterated.
FIT, OUTFIT	Equipment for injecting drugs.
FIX	To inject drugs or one dose of a particular drug; also, outfit.
FLASH	The intense feeling the user experiences just after fixing. Sudden sense of pleasure.
FLASHBACK	Re-occurrence of the drug reaction from LSD weeks to months later without taking the drug again.
FLUSH	The initial feeling the user gets when injecting a drug like methamphetamine. Sudden onrush of drug.
FOOTBALLS	Amphetamines (oval shaped) and Dilaudid.
FORWARDS	Pep pills, especially amphetamines.
FRANTIC	Nervous, jittery drug user.
FREAK	One who has flipped, i.e., one who uses drugs to the point of loss of reality; especially used as "speed freak" when referring to a heavy methedrine user.
FREAK OUT	To lose all contact with reality; to have a drug party.
FREAK TRIP	Adverse drug reaction, especially with LSD.
FUZZ	The law.
GARBAGE	Poor quality drugs.
GEEZE	Injection of drugs.
GO	To participate freely in the drug scene.
GOOD GO	A good or reliable dealer in drugs.

GOOF BALLS	Barbiturates; any barbiturate tablet or capsule; may be combined with an amphetamine. Also far out drug users.
GOOFED UP	Under the influence of barbiturates. Behaving strangely.
GOOFER	One who uses pills. All types of drugs.
GOING UP	Taking drugs for their effects; said of smoking cannabis or injecting speed, etc. Under the influence of drugs.
GIGGLE-SMOKE	Cannabis, or cannabis smoke. Marijuana.
GRASS	Marijuana in the raw state, such as leaves, stems, seeds.
GRASSHOPPER	Marijuana user.
GRASS BROWNIES	Cookies containing marijuana.
GROOVY	Good; "out of sight."
GRIFFO	Cannabis. Marijuana.
GUIDE	One who "babysits" with a novice when he goes up on a psychedelic substance and acts as a guide.
GUN	A hypodermic needle to inject drugs.
"H"	Heroin.
HABIT	Physically or psychologically dependent on drugs; addiction to drugs. Craving for drugs.
HALLUCINOGENS	*See* Psychedelics.
HAND-TO-HAND	Delivery of narcotics person-to-person.
HASH, HASHISH	Resin from the Cannabis Indica plant, which contains a very high tetrahydrocannabinol content.

HASHBURY	Haight-Ashbury, District of San Francisco.
HEAD	Chronic user of a drug or drugs.
HEARTS	Amphetamines, specifically dextro-amphetamine and benzedrine sulfate; also, dexedrine (orange-colored, heart-shaped tablets).
HEAT	A police officer, the law. Also taking drugs.
HEAVY	Significant, weighty; highly emotional. Also addictive drugs.
HIGH	Under the influence of a drug, usually a stimulant. A drug user who is "up." Exhilarated.
HIT	Dose of a drug into addict's vein.
HOG	A drug user who takes all of a drug he can get his hands on.
HOLDING	Possessing narcotics. Or any drugs.
HOOKED	Addicted; a confirmed drug abuser.
SNORTING, SNIFFING	Sniffing narcotics through nasal passages.
HYPE	One who uses intravenous drugs, specifically heroin or speed with hypodermic injection.
HYPE OUTFIT	Equipment for injecting drugs.
ICE-CREAM	Sporadic use of drugs. Infrequent use.
HABIT	Addiction to drugs.
J or JAY	Joint or marijuana cigarette.
JAR DEALER	A person who sells drugs in 1000-tablet or capsule bottles.
JOINT	A marijuana cigarette.
JOLT	An injection of narcotics.
JOY POP	Intermittent (rather than continuous) injection of one dose of a drug; also one who is joy popping takes an injection only now and

140

	then. Also used for opium smoking.
JUG	1000-tablet or capsule bottle.
JUNK	Heroin.
KEE	Kilo.
KEG	25,000 amphetamine capsules or tablets, or more.
KICK, KICKING	To stop using drugs. *See* Cold turkey.
KICKS	A drug experience.
KILO	2.2 pounds.
KIT	Same as Outfit or narcotic paraphernalia.
"L"	LSD.
LAB	Equipment used to manufacture drugs illegally.
LAID OUT	Being informed on.
LAME	Not very smart; dumb, or green.
LEAN	A nondrug user.
LID	*See* Can.
LOADED	High on drugs, under the influence of drugs.
MAGIC MUSHROOM	The Mexican species of mushroom containing psilocybin, a psychedelic.
MAINLINE	Veins of body, usually arms; also intravenous injection.
MAINLINER	One who injects narcotics directly into the veins intravenously.
MAKE IT	To buy narcotics; to leave the scene, area.
MAN (THE)	The law, or a connection (drug supplier).
MANICURE	To prepare marijuana for use in cigarettes; removing seeds and stems.

141

MARY JANE	An old term for marijuana, rarely used.
MATCHBOX	A small amount of cannabis sufficient to make between five to eight cigarettes; about a fifth of a lid.
MDA	A hallucinogen, methyl-3, 4-methylenedioxyphenethylamine.
MELLOW YELLOW	Refers to smoking banana skins, a hoax as they contain no mind-altering drugs.
MICKEY, MICKEY FINN	Chloral hydrate.
MIND BLOWER	Pure, unadulterated drugs.
MOHASKY, MU, MUGGLES	Cannabis.
MOTA	Marijuana.
MULE	A person who delivers or carries drugs for dealer.
NARCOTIC	Refers to the natural and synthetic derivatives of opium (morphine, heroin, codeine); *not* a synonym for drugs.
NARK	Narcotics agent.
NEEDLE	Hypodermic needle.
NICKEL BUY	A five-dollar purchase.
NUMBER	A joint.
O.D.	Overdose of drugs, usually heroin.
OPE	Opium.
OUT OF IT	Not in contact; not part of the drug scene.
OUT OF SIGHT	Good, groovy; a positive descriptive term.
OUTFIT, FIT	Equipment for injection by hypodermic method; a hype outfit—eyedropper and needle, spoon, pacifier, etc.

142

OWSLEY'S ACID	LSD purportedly illegally manufactured by Augustus Owsley Stanley III; also infers that it is good-quality LSD.
OZ, OUNCE	Refers to ounce of narcotics, usually heroin or meth.
PANAMA RED	A potent type of South American cannabis Marijuana from Panama.
PANIC	Refers to condition when the drug supply has been cut off (usually caused by the arrest of a big peddler); a scarcity of drugs.
PAPER	A paper of drugs.
PEACE PILL, P.C.P.	Refers to the drug phencyclidine, originally an anesthetic for dogs.
PER	A prescription.
PEZ	Candies impregnated with LSD.
PIECE	A pistol, revolver.
PIG	*See* Hog; also a police officer.
PILL HEAD, PILL FREAK, PILLY	Amphetamine or barbiturate user. An addict high on drugs. Dangerous to himself and others.
POINT	Hypodermic needle.
POKE	A puff on a joint.
POP	A subcutaneous injection, usually referred to as "skin poppin'."
POPPER	Amyl nitrate in ampule form, inhaled.
POT; POTHEAD	Marijuana user.
POT LIKKER	Cannabis tea, usually made with regular tea boiled with cannabis leaves.
POWDER	Amphetamine powder.
PSYCHEDELIC	Means a drug whose actions primarily affect the mind; i.e., "mind-

	manifesting" (LSD, marijuana, etc.).
PUSHER	Drug peddler to users; one who seeks more business from regular customers.
PUT DOWN	To stop taking drugs.
QUARTER	Quarter of an ounce of either heroin or meth, usually four to eight grams.
RAINBOWS	Tuinal (amobarbital sodium and secobarbital sodium).
RED, REDS, RED BIRDS, RED DEVILS	Seconal (secobarbital sodium).
REDS & BLUES	Tuinal. Blue and orange color.
REEFER	Marijuana cigarette.
REGISTER	To wait until blood comes into the hypodermic before injecting a drug intravenously.
RIGHTEOUS	Good-quality drugs.
RIP OFF	To forcibly rob a peddler of his drugs or money or both.
ROACH	Small butt of marijuana cigarette.
ROLL, ROLL DECK	A tin-foil wrapped roll of tablets.
ROLL DEALER	A person who sells tablets in rolls.
RUN	To take drugs continuously for at least three days.
RUSH	*See* Flash.
SCORE, SCORING	Make a drug purchase. Also proceeds of a robbery by an addict.
SCRIPT	Drug prescription.
SHOOTING GALLERY	Place where users can purchase drugs and inject them; place where an injection of a drug can be used and/or bought.
SHOOT UP	To inject drugs.

144

SHOT	An injection of a drug.
SKIN POPPING	Intramuscular or subcutaneous injection of drugs.
SLEEPERS	A depressant-type drug such as barbiturates.
SMACK	Heroin.
SMASHED	Intoxicated, stoned, high.
SNIFFING, SNORTING,	Using narcotics by sniffing through nasal passages, usually heroin or cocaine.
SNITCH	Informer, stoolie.
SNOW	Cocaine.
SNOWBIRD	Cocaine user.
SOURCE	Where narcotics are obtained; supplier such as pusher, dealer, connection.
SPACE OUT, SPACED	In a daze, particularly a daze resulting from a trip due to use of drugs.
SPATZ	Capsules.
SPEED	Methedrine (methamphetamine) or crystal; now-broadened use in some areas to mean any amphetamine or any stimulant.
SPEED FREAKS	*See* Freak.
SPEEDBALL	A powerful shot of a drug, usually heroin and cocaine combined.
SPIKE	Hypodermic needle.
SPLASH	Speed.
SPLIT	To leave, flee, break up with.
SPOON	A quantity of heroin, theoretically measured on a teaspoon (usually between one and two grams), sixteen spoons per ounce.
SQUARE	A person who does not know what's happening, a nonuser.

STANLEY'S STUFF	LSD purportedly manufactured by Augustus Owsley Stanley III. *See* Owsley's acid.
STASH	Place where narcotic or outfit is hidden; also, refers to one's own supply of drugs.
STONED	Under the influence of drugs.
STOOLIE	Informer. *See* Snitch.
STP	Serenity, tranquility, peace—a drug mixture of methedrine and psychedelic compounds (4-Methyl 2, 5 Dimethoxy Alpha Methyl Phenethylamine), DOM-hallucinogenic drug.
STRAIGHT (TEEN MEANING)	Under the influence of narcotics; applied to a peddler, gives a good deal.
STRUNG OUT	Heavily addicted or hooked.
STUFF	General term for drugs and narcotics.
SYNDICATE ACID	STP.
TASTE	A small sample of a narcotic.
TD CAPS	Time-disintegrating capsules.
TEA	Cannabis, marijuana.
TOKE UP	To light a marijuana cigarette.
TORN UP	Intoxicated, stoned.
TRACKS	A series of puncture wounds in the veins caused by continued narcotic injections. Appears on skin of addict as tracks.
TRAVEL AGENT	A pusher of hallucinogenic drugs.
TREY	A three-dollar purchase.
TRIGGER	To smoke a marijuana cigarette immediately after taking LSD.
TRIP	The hallucinations and/or feelings experienced by a person after taking a drug, particularly LSD.

TURN ON	To use drugs, or to introduce another person to the use of drugs.
TURN ON, TUNE IN, DROP OUT	To take LSD, learn about the "real" world, and drop out of the nondrugged world. Introducing someone to drugs.
UPPER	Amphetamine.
UPTIGHT	Angry, anxious; (may rarely be used to mean good, as in the words to a song, "Everythings uptight, out of sight.").
USER	One who uses drugs.
VIBS, VIBRATIONS	Feelings coming from another; may be good or bad vibs.
WASTED	High or drunk.
WEDGES	Small tablets shaped like wedges (almost triangular).
WEED	Marijuana.
WEED HEAD	Marijuana smoker.
WEEKEND HABIT	Irregular drug habit.
WEIRD	Drugs user. Same as freak.
WEST COAST TURN-AROUNDS	Amphetamine tablets or capsules.
WHEELS	Automobile. Transportation.
WHITES	Amphetamine tablets.
WIG OUT, WIGGING	Blow your mind. Freakout on excessive drugs. Over dosage.
WORKS	Equipment for drug injecting into user's veins.
YELLOW JACKETS, YELLOWS	Nembutal (pentobarbital sodium). Nicknamed from the yellow shade of the capsule.

LIST OF HALFWAY HOUSES
FOR DRUG INFORMATION

STATE   ADDRESS

ALABAMA

1. Alabama State   Temperance Education Division
   Department of   State Office Building
   Education   Montgomery, Alabama

2. Alabama State   Alcohol Narcotics Division
   Department of   State Office Building
   Health   Montgomery, Alabama

ARIZONA

3. Awareness House   P. O. Box 17503
   C. J. Alexander,   Tucson, Arizona 85710
   M.D.
   Medical Advisor

4. Community Organiza-   1807 North Central Avenue
   tion for Drug Abuse   Phoenix, Arizona 85004
   CODAC

5. Maricopa Mental   341 West McDowell Road
   Health Association   Phoenix, Arizona 85003

ARKANSAS

6. The Drug Abuse   University of Arkansas
   Educational   Medical Center
   Program   Little Rock, Arkansas 72201

CALIFORNIA

7. American Indian   526 East Oaks Street
   Free Clinic   Compton, California 90220

8. American Social   785 Market Street
   Health Association   San Francisco, California 94103

9. Berkeley Free Clinic 2418 Haste Street
                         Berkeley, California 94704

10. California Drug   Department of Pharmacology
    Abuse Information   University of California
    Committee   Medical Center
                          San Francisco, California 94122

11. Drug Abuse Research   UCLA Neuropsychiatric
    and Education   Institute
    Foundation   UCLA Campus
                          Los Angeles, California 90024

12. Haight Ashbury-Free   558 Clayton Street
    Clinic   San Francisco, California 94117

13. Los Angeles Free   115 North Fairfax Avenue
    Clinic, Inc.   Los Angeles, California 90036

14. Mendocino State   P. O. Box X
    Hospital Drug   Talmage, California 95481
    Abuse Treatment
    Program

15. Synanon Foundation,   1910 Ocean Front
    Inc.   Santa Monica, California 90405

                          1215 Clay Street
                          Oakland, California 94612

COLORADO

16. Colorado Council on Drug Abuse Information and Education, Inc.

P. O. Box 6004
Denver, Colorado 80206

17. Colorado State Department of Health

Alcoholism and Dependence
Division
4210 East 11th Avenue
Denver, Colorado 80220

18. Colorado State University Student Health Center

Fort Collins, Colorado 80521

19. United States Bureau Narcotics and Dangerous Drugs

Denver Office
1814 California Street
Denver, Colorado 80202

CONNECTICUT

20. Connecticut State Department of Mental Health Alcohol and Drug Dependence Division

51 Coventry Street
Hartford, Connecticut 06112

21. Capitol Region Drug Information Center

179 Allyn Street
Hartford, Connecticut 06103

22. Narcotics Addiction Research & Community Opportunities, Inc.

216-224 Congress Avenue
New Haven, Connecticut 06519

STATE	ADDRESS

23. Project Renaissance,   21 Taylor Place
     Inc.   Westport, Connecticut 06880

DELAWARE

24. Delaware Department   Administration Building
     of Mental Health   Delaware State Hospital
                       New Castle, Delaware 19720

25. Delaware Pharma-   Clendening Pharmacy
     ceutical Society   Harrington, Delaware 19952
     Committee on
     Drug Abuse

26. Governor's Commis-   910 Market Street
     sion on Drug Abuse   Wilmington, Delaware 19899

DISTRICT OF COLUMBIA

27. Community Addiction   1400 Q Street, N. W.
     Treatment Center   Washington, D. C. 20009

28. Drug Addiction   1825 13th Street, N. W.
     Treatment and   Washington, D. C. 20009
     Rehabilitation
     Center

29. Drug Central   1225 Connecticut Avenue,
     Metropolitan Wash-   N. W.
     ington Government   Washington, D. C. 20036
     Councils

30. Washington Free   1556 Wisconsin Avenue, N. W.
     Clinic, Inc.   Washington, D. C. 20005

STATE	ADDRESS

31. United States Bureau   14th and Eye Streets, N. W.
      of Narcotics and   Washington, D. C. 20537
      Dangerous Drugs

FLORIDA

32. The Governor's Task   325 East Gaines Street
      Force on Narcotics,   Tallahassee, Florida 32304
      Dangerous Drugs
      and Alcohol

33. Jackson Memorial   1700 N. W. 10th Avenue
      Hospital Drug   Miami, Florida 33136
      Detoxification Clinic

GEORGIA

34. American Social   173 Walton Street, N. W.
      Health Association   Atlanta, Georgia 30303

35. Emory University   1380 South Oxford Road, N. E.
      Student Drug Abuse   Atlanta, Georgia 30322
      Panel

36. Mercer University   223 Walton Street, N. W.
      Southern School of   Atlanta, Georgia 30303
      Pharmacy

37. United States Bureau   Atlanta, Georgia 30303
      of Narcotics and   1056 Federal Office Building
      Dangerous Drugs

HAWAII

38. Hawaii Council on   Aloha Tower
      Addiction   Honolulu, Hawaii 96813

STATE	ADDRESS
39. Hawaii Department of Health	P. O. Box 3378 Honolulu, Hawaii 96801
40. Hawaii Medical Association	510 South Beretania Street Honolulu, Hawaii 96813
41. Queen's Hospital	1301 Punchbowl Street Honolulu, Hawaii 96813
42. Waikiki Drug Clinic	319 Paokalani Avenue Honolulu, Hawaii 96815

IDAHO

43. Idaho Bureau of Drug Control	1203 Imperial Plaza 200 North Third Boise, Idaho 83702

ILLINOIS

44. American Medical Association (AMA) Department of Mental Health	535 North Dearborn Chicago, Illinois 60610
45. Gateway House Foundation, Inc.	4800 South Ellis Avenue Chicago, Illinois 60615
46. Illinois Drug Abuse Rehabilitation Program	57th Street—South Lake Shore Drive Chicago, Illinois 60637
47. St. Leonard's House	2100 West Warren Avenue Chicago, Illinois 60612

48. United States Bureau   1836 U. S. Courthouse
    of Narcotics and   Federal Office Building
    Dangerous Drugs   Chicago, Illinois 60604

INDIANA

49. Drug Education   1330 West Michigan
    Committee Indiana   Indianapolis, Indiana 46206
    State Board of
    Health

50. Drug Information and   802 North Lafayette Boulevard
    Referral Center   South Bend, Indiana 46601
    U.W.C.A.

51. Eli Lilly and Company   Indianapolis, Indiana 46206
    Drug Abuse
    Committee

52. Indiana Department of   1315 West 10th Street
    Mental Health   Indianapolis, Indiana 50309

IOWA

53. Mid-Iowa Drug Abuse   265 Jewelt Building
    Council (MIDAC)   Des Moines, Iowa 50309

54. Pharmacy Examiners   Valley Park Building
    Drug Abuse   Third Floor
    Division   Des Moines, Iowa 50300

KANSAS

55. The Menninger   Box 829
    Foundation   Topeka, Kansas 66601

56. University of Kansas   Rainbow Boulevard at 39th
    Medical Center   Street
    Methadone Clinic   Kansas City, Kansas 66103

KENTUCKY

57. Drug Abuse Informa-   207 West Market Street
    tion and Drug   Louisville, Kentucky 40202
    Education Center,
    Inc.

58. Kentucky Bureau of   P. O. Box 678
    Narcotics and   Frankfort, Kentucky 40601
    Drug Education
    Department of
    Health

59. NIMH Clinical   Box 2000
    Research Center   Leestown Road
    (United States Pub-   Lexington, Kentucky 40507
    lic Health Service
    Center founded in
    1935 for treatment
    and study of drug
    dependency and use
    —part of the U.S.
    Department of
    Health, Education
    and Welfare)

60. University of   Lexington, Kentucky 40506
    Kentucky Drug
    Information Center

MAINE

61. State Drug Abuse   Augusta, Maine 04330
    Council   507 Ocean Street
                              South Portland, Maine 04106

MARYLAND

62. Committee on Drug   John Hopkins University
    Education (CODE)   Baltimore, Maryland 21218
    Chaplain's Office

63. Maryland Drug Abuse   State Office Building
    Authority   Baltimore, Maryland 21201

64. National Institute of   5454 Wisconsin Avenue
    Mental Health   Chevy Chase, Maryland 20015
    Center for Studies

65. National Clearing-   5454 Wisconsin Avenue
    house for Drug   Chevy Chase, Maryland 20015
    Abuse Information

66. United States Bureau   955 Federal Building
    of Narcotics and   31 Hopkins Plaza
    Dangerous Drugs   Baltimore, Maryland 21201

MASSACHUSETTS

67. Boston State Hospital   591 Morton Street
    Drug Addiction—   Boston, Massachusetts 02124
    Rehabilitation Unit

68. Drug Abuse Section   State House
    Department of the   Room 373 A
    Massachusetts   Boston, Massachusetts 02133
    Attorney General

STATE	ADDRESS
69. Massachusetts Division of Drug Rehabilitation	80 Boylston Street Room 1201 Boston, Massachusetts 02116
70. United Community Services Drug Abuse Committee	54 Wendell Avenue Pittsfield, Massachusetts 01201
71. United States Bureau of Narcotics and Dangerous Drugs	1425 Post Office and Courthouse Building Boston, Massachusetts 02109

MICHIGAN

72. Michigan State Medical Society Committee on Alcohol and Drug Dependence	120 West Saginaw Street P. O. Box 152 East Lansing, Michigan 48823
73. Michigan State University Drug Education Project	Michigan State University East Lansing, Michigan 48823
74. Open City	4425 Second Avenue Detroit, Michigan 48233
75. Project Rehab.	722 Eastern Avenue, S. E. Grand Rapids, Michigan 49503
76. Synanon	8344 East Jefferson Avenue Detroit, Michigan 48214
77. United States Bureau of Narcotics and Dangerous Drugs	Suite 602 Federal Building Detroit, Michigan 48226

MINNESOTA

78. Minnesota State Medical Association Committee on Mental Health Subcommittee on Alcoholism and Drug Abuse

375 Jackson Street
St. Paul, Minnesota 55101

79. North Memorial Hospital Detoxification Center

3220 Lowry Avenue
Minneapolis, Minnesota 55422

80. Walk-In Counseling Center

2421 Chicago Avenue, South
Minneapolis, Minnesota 55404

MISSISSIPPI

81. Mississippi Bureau of Narcotics and Dangerous Drugs

P. O. Box 22631
Jackson, Mississippi 39205

82. Mississippi State Hospital

Whitfield, Mississippi 39193

MISSOURI

83. Metropolitan Kansas City Abuse Information Center

406 West 94th Street
Suite 412
Kansas City, Missouri 64111

84. Missouri Alcoholism and Drug Abuse Program

722 Jefferson
Jefferson City, Missouri 65101

STATE	ADDRESS

85. Narcotic Addiction Treatment Program (NATP) Missouri Institute of Psychiatry (3 treatment centers)

5400 Arsenal Street
St. Louis, Missouri 63139

410 North Boyle
St. Louis, Missouri 63155

5650 Pershing
St. Louis, Missouri 63155

NEBRASKA

86. Nebraska Department of Health Division of Health Education

1005 Capitol Building
Lincoln, Nebraska 68509

NEVADA

87. State of Nevada Division of Narcotics and Dangerous Drugs

Capitol
Carson City, Nevada 89701

NEW HAMPSHIRE

88. Concord Area Drug Action Committee

P. O. Box 667
Concord, New Hampshire 03301

89. New Hampshire Program on Alcohol and Drug Abuse

Twitchell Building
105 Pleasant Street
Concord, New Hampshire 03301

NEW JERSEY

90. Bureau of Narcotic Addiction and Drug Abuse	167 West Hanover Street Trenton, New Jersey 08608
91. Division of Drug Abuse Department of Public Health	65 Bergen Street Newark, New Jersey 07107
92. Integrity House	45 Lincoln Park Newark, New Jersey 07102
93. Middlesex County Aftercare Drug Addiction Clinic	Roosevelt Hospital Box 151 Metuchen, New Jersey 08840
94. Narcotics Addict Rehabilitation Center Organization	1705 Artic Avenue Atlantic City, New Jersey 08401
95. New Jersey Regional Drug Abuse Agency (six offices)	P. O. Box 4099 Bergen Station Jersey City, New Jersey 07305
	54 Spruce Street Newark, New Jersey 07102
	154 Broadway Newark, New Jersey 07102
	350 Johnson Avenue Jersey City, New Jersey 07303
	507 26th Street Union City, New Jersey 07087
	802 Main Street Asbury Park, New Jersey 07712

96. Union County
    Narcotics Clinic

43 Rahway Avenue
Elizabeth, New Jersey 07200

NEW MEXICO

97. Narcotic Addiction
    Rehabilitation Act
    Methadone Main-
    tenance Program

Bernillio County
Mental Health Center
Albuquerque, New Mexico
87105

98. Quebrar

West Mesa Radar Site
Albuquerque, New Mexico
87105

NEW YORK

99. New York State
    Narcotic Addiction
    Control Commission
    (NACC)

Executive Park East
Stuyvesant Plaza
Albany, New York 12203
and
1855 Broadway
New York, New York 10023

100. Addiction Services
     Agency of New
     York City (ASA)

71 Worth Street
New York, New York 10013

101. Addicts Rehabilitation
     Center (ARC)

253 West 123rd Street
New York, New York 10027

102. Central Harlem
     Rehabilitation
     Center

2238 Fifth Avenue
New York, New York 10037

103. Daytop Village, Inc.
     Administrative
     Offices

184 Fifth Avenue
New York, New York 10010

RESIDENTIAL CENTERS (NEW YORK & NEW JERSEY)

1. 450 Bayview Avenue
   Staten Island, New York 10309
2. 225 West 14th Street
   New York, New York 10011
3. Route 55
   Swan Lake, New York 12783
4. Day Care and Community Centers
   175 Chrystie Street
   New York, New York 10002
5. 408 East 10th Street
   New York, New York 10009
6. 431 Princeton Avenue
   Trenton, New Jersey 08619
7. 1 East 2nd Street
   Mount Vernon, New York 10801

104.	Exodus House, Inc.	304 E. 103rd Street New York, New York 10029
105.	Institute for the Study of Drug Addiction	680 West End Avenue New York, New York 10025
106.	National Association for Prevention of Addiction to Narcotics	520 First Avenue New York, New York 10016
107.	New York Association Voluntary Agencies on Narcotics Addiction and Substance Abuse (NYANA)	55 W. 14th Street New York, New York 10011
108.	New York State Addiction Control Commission	1855 Broadway New York, New York

STATE	ADDRESS

109. Odyssey House (O.H.)   309-11 East Sixth Street
                            New York, New York 10023

110. Phoenix House   205 West 85th Street
                     New York, New York 10024

111. Synanon   35 Riverside Drive
               New York, New York 10023

112. United States Bureau   90 Church Street
     Narcotics and   New York, New York 10007
     Dangerous Drugs

NORTH CAROLINA

113. North Carolina   P. O. Box 26327
     Department Mental   Raleigh, North Carolina 27611
     Health

NORTH DAKOTA

114. Foundation on Abuse   P. O. Box 2404
     of Drugs (FAD)   Fargo, North Dakota 58102

OHIO

115. Cincinnati Free Clinic,   2444 Vine Street
     Inc. (C.F.C.)   Cincinnati, Ohio 45219

116. Drug Information   Department of Medicine—J-4
     Center (DIC)   Cincinnati, Ohio 46229
     Cincinnati General
     Hospital

117. The Free Clinic   2039 Cornell Road
                      Cleveland, Ohio 44106

163

118. Talbert House

2316 Auburncrest
Cincinnati, Ohio 45219

OREGON

119. Alcohol & Drug
Section
Mental Health
Division

309 S. W. 4th Avenue
Portland, Oregon 97204

120. Outside-In
Socio-Medical Aid
Station, Inc.

1240 S. W. Salmon Street
Portland, Oregon 97205

PENNSYLVANIA

121. Philadelphia Drug
Abuse Council

1610 Spruce Street
Philadelphia, Pennsylvania
19103

122. Smith, Kline and
French

1500 Spring Garden Street
Philadelphia, Pennsylvania
19101

123. Western Pennsylvania
Council on Drug
Abuse

523 North Homewood Avenue
Pittsburgh, Pennsylvania 15208

RHODE ISLAND

124. Marathon House, Inc.

Fish Hill Road
Coventry, Rhode Island 02816

125. Together, Inc.

P. O. Box 996
Annex Station
Providence, Rhode Island
02901

SOUTH DAKOTA

126. Office of the Commissioner of Drugs and Substance Control

Office of the Attorney General
Pierre, South Dakota 57501

TENNESSEE

127. Dangerous Drugs Foundation

Chuckey, Tennessee 37647

TEXAS

128. Co-Ordinating Committee on Drug Abuse

1618 Houston
Laredo, Texas 78040

129. Corpus Christi Drug Abuse Council

425 South Broadway
Corpus Christi, Texas 78401

130. Texas Alcohol Narcotics Education, Inc. (TANE)

2814 Oak Lawn
Dallas, Texas 75219

131. United States Bureau of Narcotics and Dangerous Drugs

1114 Commerce Street
Dallas, Texas 75207

132. University YMCA-YWCA Drug Center "Middle Earth"

2200 Guadalupe
Austin, Texas 78705

UTAH

133. Community Drug
Crisis Center
(Crisis)

215 Edison Street
Salt Lake City, Utah 84111

134. State of Utah
Department of
Drug Control

Governor's Office
State Capitol Building
Salt Lake City, Utah 84101

VERMONT

135. Drug Rehabilitation
Commission (DRC)
Vermont State
Hospital

Waterbury, Vermont 05676

136. University of Vermont
Dart Research
Project Department
of Psychiatry

Burlington, Vermont 05401

137. Vermont State
Medical Society
Special Committee
on Drug Abuse

P. O. Box 68
Williston, Vermont 05495

VIRGINIA

138. Alexandria Commu-
nity Mental Health
Center-Narcotic
Addiction Programs

720 North—Asaph Streets
Alexandria, Virginia 22314

139. Peninsula Association
for Mental Health
on Drug Abuse

3015 West Avenue
Newport News, Virginia 23607

STATE	ADDRESS
140. United Drug Abuse Commission	4981 Doziers Corner Road Chesapeake, Virginia 23320

141. Drug Abuse Information Service Department of Pharmacology School of Medicine —University of Washington

Seattle, Washington 98105

142. Center for Addiction Services City of Seattle

Seattle, Washington 98104

143. Open Door Clinic

5012 Roosevelt Way N. E. Seattle, Washington 98105

144. Narcotics Center of Tacoma-Pierce County

1138 Commerce Street Tacoma, Washington 98402

WEST VIRGINIA

145. Council for Drug Information Harrison County

P. O. Box 987 Clarksburg, West Virginia 26301

WISCONSIN

146. The A Center

2000 Domanik Drive Racine, Wisconsin 53404

147. Dane County Mental Health Center Ad hoc Committee on Drug Abuse

31 South Mills Street
Madison, Wisconsin 53705

148. Dialogue on Drugs Dane County Mental Health Association

406 North Pinchney
Madison, Wisconsin 53703

149. Drug Abuse and Addiction Committee

8307 47th Avenue
Kenosha, Wisconsin 53140

150. Drug Information Group, Incorporated

824 6th Street
Racine, Wisconsin 53403

151. Special Committee on Narcotics and Drug Education of the County Board of Supervisors

Milwaukee, Wisconsin 53202

152. University of Wisconsin Drug Education Program and Information

167 Bascom Hall
Madison, Wisconsin 53706

153. Wisconsin Bureau of Alcoholism and Drug Abuse— Division Mental Hygiene Division of Health and Social Services

1 West Wilson Street
Madison, Wisconsin 53704

STATE	ADDRESS

154. Wisconsin State   Winnebago, Wisconsin 54985
      Medical Society
      Division of Alcohol-
      ism and Addiction
      Winnebago State
      Hospital

WYOMING

155. Drug Abuse Rehabili-   Evanston, Wyoming 82930
       tation Program For
   Youth
   Wyoming State Hospital

156. Fremont Counseling   195 North 4th Street
      Services   Lander, Wyoming 82520

157. Park County   1253 Sheridan Avenue
      Counseling Services   Cody, Wyoming 82414

The following dialogue, reproduced with permission of the American Broadcasting Company, is a poignant example of the tragic affect of drug abuse on our youth.

FROM "THE WESTPORT DRUG STORY"
THE ABC EVENING NEWS, FEBRUARY 26, 1971
PRODUCER: CAROLYN RUSSELL
CORRESPONDENT: SCOTT OSBORNE

VIDEO	AUDIO
Osborne on camera.	Westport, Connecticut, one of a string of wealthy suburban towns north of New York . . . the kind of place a successful business executive would choose to bring up his children. But even in Westport there is that modern sense that something's wrong . . . which can lead to drugs.
"Voice-over" narration of shots of groups of students outside Westport's Staples High School.	Westport police say they have no way of knowing how many young people use drugs, but we were told that as many as four out of five are on some kind of drug . . . from pot, to pills, to heroin.
Various shots of residential Westport,	(First Girl) "It's a dull town, and most of my friends were getting

170

and of commuters boarding train. (Voice of two teen-age Westport girls.)

into it. At first, you know, we started out drinking at parties, and like it seemed like nobody could have a good time together unless they were drunk or stoned or something, and it's pretty sad." (Second girl) "Parents don't want to believe that their children are taking drugs . . . so a lot of people are ignorant."

Various shots of members of Renaissance Project during a meeting in project house. (Osborne narration continues.)

In Westport, a program called Project Renaissance was begun two years ago by concerned citizens who called in experts . . . ex-drug addicts from New York. They realized that drug abuse is no longer an exclusive sickness of the inner city. At Project Renaissance, young drug users try to determine why they need drugs. The shock treatment you are about to witness may seem brutal, but the program organizers, who have all been through the same thing themselves, say this is the most effective way to get at the root of the problems that turn these young people to drugs. On a recent night, a sixteen-year-old named Phil Phillips was the subject. Why did Phil need drugs to maintain a strong façade? Why does he still need to come on so strong?

Shots of encounter group during which this night's subject, Phil Phillips, is attacked by fellow members, and soon reduced to uncontrollable sobbing.

(Boy) "You know, Phil, the other night you were talking like really hostile . . . like you were coming out of a hole in your neck you just couldn't believe, you know? And like you want people to show you concern . . . You want that phony kind of concern, too? You want people to come . . . up phony to you?

(Phil) "I didn't feel it was phony . . . like it could . . . you know. . . ."

(Boy) Garbled

Phil begins to cry.

(Phil) "Like in what I say . . . I told you, like I just want to stand up and be able to say things . . . and be able to do it like most of the time . . . you know."

(Girl) "How do you feel in your home?"

(Phil) "I feel like really out of place sometimes. . . ."

(Girl) "How come?"

(Phil) " 'Cause all my friends . . . it's not like all are my age, you know . . . they're all older than me . . . they all know more than me . . . they're not like the people I see from Renaissance."

172

(Girl) "How about the night when Peter said everybody here would like to thank you . . . meaning . . . (Garbled as all begin talking.)

(Phil, sobbing openly) "It got me really uptight . . got me uptight . . . I want to belong!!"

Shots of Phil crying and of other members of group as Osborne's voice concludes story.

No one leaves a session like the one you have just seen until he is once again in control of his emotions . . . And the Renaissance directors firmly believe that all leave with a little better understanding of what got them on drugs in the first place. The problems of Westport, Connecticut, are not unique among upper-middle-class communities. What Westport has that is different is Project Renaissance . . . an attempt to get at those problems. Scott Osborne, ABC News, Westport, Connecticut.